FAITH BEYOND BELIEF
A Journey to Freedom

FAITH BEYOND BELIEF
A Journey to Freedom

David Eberly

Brandylane Publishers, Inc.
www.brandylanepublishers.com
1711 East Main Street, Suite 9
Richmond, Virginia 23223
804.644.3090 or 1.800.553.6922
email: *brandy@crosslink.net*

Cover concept by Tom Hale Studios

Library of Congress Cataloging-in-Publication Data

Eberly, David, 1947-
    Faith beyond belief : a journey to freedom / David Eberly.
        p. cm.
Originally published: Richmond, Va. : Brandylane Publishers, 2002.
    ISBN 1-883911-47-8
    1. Eberly, David, 1947- 2. Persian Gulf War, 1991--Personal
narratives, American. 3. Prisoners of war--United States--Biography.
4. Airmen--United States--Biography. I. Title.

DS79.74.E24 2003
956.7044'27--dc21

                                        2003010494

To Barbara,
the wind beneath my wings.

TABLE OF CONTENTS

FOREWORD

Christian faith is based on an acceptance of God's promise to care for us throughout eternity. In troubled times, when life is defined by the moment, we must trust His grace and confide in our faith to find the inner strength and courage to face our deepest fears or to overcome the most challenging tragedies. By intense example this spellbinding story of combat survival demonstrates the power of unquestioned faith.

Faith Beyond Belief is the captivating testimony of personal faith by the senior allied prisoner of the Gulf War. Colonel Eberly's dramatic recollection puts you in his F-15E cockpit at shootdown, in the Iraqi desert evading the enemy, and witness to a lifetime in the cold dark damp cells of Baghdad. No one has explained more intensely the paralyzing experience of being hit by an exploding enemy missile, the agony of capture, and the dismal isolation and starvation of Saddam's grasp. You walk with David through the Valley of the Shadow of Death and along his journey to freedom.

This book profoundly reflects the importance of faith and focus in life. It is a powerful story for believers and nonbelievers, for young and old, and for all that may ever doubt God's everlasting love. Its uplifting message renews His promise to everyone that the Lord is our Shepherd—He is always on guard.

Dr. Robert Schuller
The Crystal Cathedral

PREFACE

This is one of God's war stories, a story of faith, faith beyond belief. It is the parable of His love woven through the lyrics of hymns like "Amazing Grace," "Faith of our Fathers," and "What a Friend We Have in Jesus."

The story of my experience began with a brilliant white flash. Then, somewhere through a black hole in the night, I entered another lifetime, a seemingly endless moment possibly not unlike the experience of others who are tested and whose faith is measured. Once again we know the ageless promise of His care for a fallen sparrow and the old, old story of Jesus and his love. I have written of my journey with the Lord to witness to his Word: *I am with you all the days of your life.*

On the fourth night of the Gulf War, His hand saved me when my fighter aircraft was hit by an Iraqi surface-to-air missile. He took the pain from my injuries and cleared my mind, enabling me to avoid immediate capture. Once reunited with my backseater, we evaded the enemy for three nights until we were captured near the Iraqi border while attempting to escape to Syria. During my subsequent 43 days as a prisoner of war, the Lord was my shepherd. He was my constant companion, the source of my strength and my courage. He answered my prayers, and he kept me sane. On His time, He led us home.

The families of those "missing-in-action" during the war with Iraq, just as with other wars and military actions, endured the toughest times imaginable. For the spouses, the moms and dads, the sons and daughters, the brothers and sisters, and the friends, facing the unknown, day after day, tested their faith. Contrary to the protocols of the Geneva Convention, no information (with the exception of propaganda video) was released by the Iraqi government on the missing allied military personnel, no lists of captured airmen were ever passed to the International Committee of the Red Cross, nor did Saddam identify or allow any inspection of the prisons where POWs were held.

At Seymour Johnson AFB, Barbara, my wife, and Timm, our son, were surrounded by the love of friends, the support of the local community of Goldsboro, North Carolina, and the prayers from thousands of people across the country and around the world. In Brazil, Indiana, my mother and stepfather felt the same out-pouring of support. Both Timm and my mother, Evelyn Wallace, hundreds of miles apart, shared the vision of me "walking in the desert" as I evaded the enemy that first night. They, too, felt God's comforting hand; their faith helped ease the heartbreak of tragedy.

As a family, we owe thanks today to the strong leadership of President George H.W. Bush. On February 2, 1991, within two weeks of my shootdown, he came to Seymour Johnson AFB to visit Barbara and the families of the other POW/MIAs. In private conversations, he told them his first priority would be the return of the prisoners. History reflects he was true to his word.

The twenty-one Americans returned to Andrews AFB on Sunday, March 10, 1991. I began my brief remarks to those gathered and those watching around the world on CNN, with these words: "God saved us. Our families' love and your prayers sustained us, and for many, the camaraderie of our flying squadrons brought us home to fly again."

As a result of this experience, I am not afraid of dying—I am afraid of not appreciating living. The greatest struggle in our busy lives is to take time to be holy—to put the Lord first. We cannot know, or even imagine the challenges and the opportunities that God will give us each day. We must simply have faith; He is with us always. Our shepherd is on guard.

ACKNOWLEDGEMENTS

One song, *Voices That Care,* best reflects the spirit of the American people during the Fall of 1990, and, became the anthem for the renewed patriotism felt by those who "cheered their heroes on" during the trials of Desert Storm.

We heard your voices; we read your love letters; and, we felt your prayers. From the boardrooms, living rooms and classrooms, your cards, care packages and the children's drawings showed that this time you cared about the soldiers, sailors, airmen, and Marines serving so far from home.

Thank you.

INTRODUCTION

by General Chuck Horner, USAF (Ret)

In August 1990, thousands of Americans were deployed with little warning to Saudi Arabia and other nations in the Middle East to stop the Iraqi invasion. They were not asked to volunteer nor could they expect little but brutal hot days, miserable food and the opportunity to be wounded or killed. As the days became weeks and months, their will was tested. It was not known when they could return to their families. Their living conditions improved only marginally and their life in an alien land offered few of the off-duty diversions Americans take for granted. Still they served, selflessly, with great competence and dedication. Their morale never waned, despite great loneliness and longing for home and loved ones. Then in late November, it became apparent that there would be a war to liberate occupied Kuwait, and all thoughts of self-pity were buried under the burden of preparing for combat.

On the eve of war, all of us were filled with apprehension, not so much out of fear for our own lives although there was plenty of reason for such thoughts given the size of the enemy we faced. Our minds were instead filled with thoughts of those who would die because of our actions. Commanders worried about mistakes they might make that would cost the lives of their men and women. All of us lived with the dread that no matter how carefully we planned and executed our air attacks, Iraqis would die. While it was reasonable to justify the death of the murderers who were raping Kuwait and its people, we, Christians, Jews, and Muslims alike, entered this war with a very heavy heart.

When the deadline for Iraq to withdraw from occupied Kuwait came and went, our apprehension turned to grim determination. Those of us who had never experienced combat feared failure more than death. Those who had seen tracers slip by their aircraft's canopy wondered about the odds of their returning home from one more war. But all of the coalition entered the fray; we were the best trained and best equipped airman ever assembled in behalf of a noble cause. We used our minds and our consciences seeking to avoid the loss of even a single life. Of course, we failed. But, our trying was not in vain as losses were lighter on both sides than ever recorded in history for a war of such magnitude. Nonetheless, some were killed and wounded and others spent time captive in the hands of our evil adversary.

This is a story of an American who was shot down, wounded and imprisoned by the Iraqis. It is a story that is spell binding and inspirational. It reminds me of the faith that sustained the Apostle Paul during his ordeal in prison. In this case it is a story of Colonel Dave Eberly, the most senior officer captured by the Iraqis who had to carry his own burdens while shouldering responsibility for all the other coalition prisoners held in Baghdad.

His story demonstrates how fragile our earthly existence can be, how one moment all is well and then you are struggling to maintain life itself, fighting to retain your sanity, confronted with what could become paralyzing fear. To be sure, he had been trained to withstand these forces, but no training can adequately prepare one for the hell on earth that Dave was forced to endure. There is only one remedy for moments in life such at this: faith. He was thrust into an existence that only his faith in God could provide him the strength needed to survive, to remain sane, to lead so that others could survive. Veterans often reject the concept of heroes because they know well their own fears, nonetheless they admire heroic actions of others. Dave Eberly may or may not be a hero, but he was thrust into a situation where heroic action was required. He was motivated and sustained by his own faith in God; his success is a tribute to faith. His experiences provide an inspiring message for all of us.

(General Horner was the allied air component commander of the Gulf War and co-authored *Every Man A Tiger* with Tom Clancy.)

PROLOGUE

Thursday, August 9, 1990, was a day charged with excitement. For the families of the airmen at Seymour Johnson AFB, the invasion by Saddam Hussein into the Saudi Arabian peninsula one week earlier forever changed the lives of many who deployed to the Persian Gulf for Operation Desert Shield.

Barbara's parting words as I left home for the flightline were: "you've waited 20 years for this."

Stepping to the jets in the heavy rain, we could see the absolute pride in the eyes and actions of every waiting crew chief. * For them, this engine start was like the "big show" in the movie *Bull Durham.* Engine rotation, fuel flow, and ignition were methodically followed by systems and flight control checks, radio check in, and finally the visual signal to pull the wheel chocks. As our heavily loaded Eagle moved forward, the crew chief gave me a thumbs-up, and as blowing rain beat him in the face, he stood smartly at attention as we exchanged customary salutes. Along the taxiway at base operations, the families, also soaked by the driving rain, stood huddled under

---

* Also on the rain soaked ramp that morning was Chaplain Ray Hart. Ray is an airman's pastor. Standing ankle-deep in blowing water, he was there, as always, not as a cheerleader but as a shepherd. I knew he wanted to come along but for now only his words, "God be with you" would go with us.

flapping umbrellas—cheering their heroes on. The KC-10 tankers took off first. Then the fighters were sequenced onto the runway and cleared for takeoff. Ironically, the torrential rainstorms that pounded our North Carolina base that morning cast the players for the Desert Storm that culminated the historic deployment of US military forces to Southwest Asia.

From the flightline, Barbara and Timm drove home and went on with life and plans for his first year of college. I had told her I might not be back in time to help move him to Wilmington but that I would be back in time for parents weekend at UNCW in early September. How naïve we were to the events of the next seven months.

The long thirteen and a half hour flight was filled with challenge. Of the twenty-eight fighters that launched, including four spares, only twenty-two landed in Saudi Arabia and of those only eighteen could continue to our final destination in Oman.

The first to divert was Lt Col "Rusty" Bolt, the squadron commander. After joining with the tankers just off the East Coast, he moved into position under the air-refueling probe to check his air refueling system. When the boomer plugged him, his left wing tank seemed to explode, and he began to trail raw fuel before quickly disconnecting. This valve seal problem accounted for most of our airborne spare substitutions and would have resulted in other over-water diversions except that my backseater, "Two Dogs" McIntyre figured out an alternative for fuel transfer.

Later, around midnight at approximately 1,000 miles west of the Azores, we also had two fuel tanks blow out. And then, as we transited the Mediterranean, we were advised through the tankers that we had been denied landing approval at our planned deployment base. Still, without sacrificing safety, I was determined to continue and to get as many fighters into the theater as possible. Like the trail boss from a cattle drive in the old West, I felt responsible for bringing them into town. Fate was no match for my determination.

For the team of aviators, maintainers, and base support personnel from the Fourth Tactical Fighter Wing, the opportunities and leadership challenges that lay ahead were far beyond our imagination. The rapid build up of forces over the next couple weeks in the theater and at our new home at Thumrait, Oman, was awesome. Two actions reflected the seriousness of the National Command Authority: the call-up of the 200K reserve force and the activation of the Civil Reserve Air Fleet (CRAF). * Flights arrived minutes apart around the clock bringing supplies into our remote staging area and taxed the in-theater cargo mission of our co-located C-130 wing. For the aircrews, the hours became days and the days became months. We lived on the edge of readiness—waiting for the launch order, grasping for every hint of action. The harsh desert environment brought a new dimension to our combat training.

Back home the families endured the same emotional roller coaster. Vietnam-like demonstrations and over-publicized complaints by some activated Guard and Reserve persons got international media attention. Some found it inconceivable that they might ever have to really go to war; some lost faith in our national leaders and tried to value freedom in terms of cents per gallon. Having forgotten the lessons from

---

* The CRAF activation takes commercial airline aircraft for military deployment flights.

WWII, most cared little about a country smaller than the state of New Hampshire or a land so far away.

By late October, Timm lost complete focus on his studies and renewed his thoughts to "go help Dad." Barbara's premonition led her to shop for a simple navy dress.

The November 29th UN Security Council resolution formally authorized the use of force and set a final date for Saddam to withdraw. Additional forces were identified and plans were finalized to accommodate additional aircraft. To alleviate some of the air refueling requirements, we moved the wing from Thumrait to a new expansive bare base in Saudi where we were joined by a second F-15E squadron from Seymour, an F-15C squadron from Bitberg, Germany, and two F-16 units from Air National Guard units in South Carolina and New Jersey.

Al Kharj, located South of Riyadh, had ten million square feet of concrete but nothing else. Until the expansive tent city was built by Colonel Ray Davies and the Red Horse civil engineering team, the tallest structure was a taxiway light— no water, no electrical power, and no fuel storage.

As the UN deadline approached, we waited for final orders. Personally, I hoped the world would not suffer an excuse in Saddam's propaganda to extend the ultimatum for his withdrawal of occupying forces in Kuwait. At Al Kharj the Pentagon press pool including Bob Simon (CBS), Michael Hedges *(The Washington Times)*, and Edie Leherer (AP) questioned our resolve and readiness as the deadline approached. "We don't anticipate dates," I said. "We anticipate the next sortie." I was proud of what our team had done; I was confident of our training.

Tuesday, January 15th was a quiet day in the desert. The

aviators took a day of rest while Ray and the maintenance guys readied the one hundred plus fighters for The Big Show. It was a beautiful day with blue skies, calm winds and ideal for a run and workout or a game of volleyball. Many wrote letters home. Sometime after noon we got the launch message and the initial 24-hour sortie frag for Desert Storm. In less than thirty-six hours the F-15E Strike Eagles would enter combat for the first time.

The first night. A professional quietness permeated the tent city on Wednesday, the 16th as everyone prepared for the late night launch. There had been no official announcement to the support personnel but it was obvious that the rehearsal was over. I don't remember much about the flight briefing; I do remember the well wishes of the support folks. As "Two Dogs" and I approached our aircraft on the dimly lit ramp I recognized the familiar silhouette of my friend, Chaplain Ray Hart. Ray was walking the line, adding his prayers for "God's speed." We were finally going to do it. Everyone knew they were about to be part of history; every airman had put his and her professional best into preparing for this next engine start. Their hearts pounded with the thunder of the takeoff, and their spirits flew with the trailing blue orange afterburner plume of the departing fighters. No one, especially the aircrews, focused on the daunting statistic that up to ten percent of the initial strike force could be lost to enemy fire.

Coming off the tanker, we began a calculated descent to avoid detection by Iraqi early warning radar. Leveling off at 200 feet and now just minutes from crossing the border, I was actually relieved that we were beyond recall by the command authority to abort the strike. Our ingress flight path took us directly over the two enemy radar sites North of Ar Ar. In the black void through the HUD* I saw two fires ahead on the horizon and knew our special helicopter force had opened the door.

Approaching the target area, SCUD missile sites at H-3 airbase, I cracked the afterburner and started a quick climb to 21,000 feet to avoid the perimeter missile threat. Ahead, at left 11-oclock, all the airfield lights burned brightly. I couldn't believe my eyes. He doesn't know we're coming, I thought. Then it started. The sky below us lit up. "Two Dogs" had masterfully refined the target presentation; my thumb decisively depressed the bomb button on the stick grip—releasing six five hundred-pound bombs. "We're out of here," I said as I turned right, then rolled inverted to dive back to the surface to egress at low altitude. Headed south, I was conscious of flight members ahead but pushed it up to near supersonic. Our silence was broken as "Two Dogs" identified "bandits" slightly high on the nose. Then to my right, a splash and moments later, another. The two Iraqi fighters exploded as they hit the ground.

After crossing the border we rejoined a tanker, refueled and continued South to recover at Al Kharj. The welcome was incredible. Lining the back of the parking ramp the support troops were unabashedly cheering and waving as the flights of fighters taxied in. Silently, I repeated my earlier prayer. Thank you, God…we made it.

Thursday, as CNN and the world press reported on

---

* Our LANTIRN projection on the heads-up-display was inoperative. Normally the HUD display would have shown a real-time computer-generated daylight view of the terrain ahead. Since coming off the tanker we had tried unsuccessfully to recycle the system. On any other night we would have aborted.

the first night's strikes, Barbara joined other wives for a press conference at Seymour Johnson. "Barb said she was a little concerned as the sounds of war began on television, but she wasn't worried," reported a News-Argus staff writer under the headline "Wives of Pilots from Seymour Wait, Pray." "We hope, pray, and don't worry till we get word," she added.

I didn't get much sleep the next couple days other than an unintentional catnap at the command post. "Steep" Turner, Steve Pingle, "Bigs" and the other squadron commanders had also flown the first night and then folded into the flow while carefully monitoring their aircrew's schedule. I tried to keep focused on the tasking, but also wanted to get short debriefs from returning crews. Sadly, the second night an F-15E flight lead brought the disheartening news that a wingman was unaccounted for. From the black smoke in the video of a trailing fighter it was apparently possible that the aircraft might have gone in just off the target. It was a painful reminder of the price of war.

Barbara had planned to visit our friends, the Vineyards, in Williamsburg starting Friday, but canceled her trip and called Ann to ask her to come to Seymour. "I couldn't stand the long drive home alone when something happened to David," she said. Then, at noon she called her Uncle Ed in Buffalo. "If something happens, will you come?"

Late Friday afternoon I saw Grif * in the 335th squad-

* Major Tom Griffith and I had been friends since we first met in the early 80s while flying F-4Es at Ramstein AB Germany. In the late 80s, Grif was selected for a special headquarters intern program and assigned in my office at the Pentagon. In 1990, we again met at Seymour Johnson AFB, NC where he was among the first to transition to the new F-15E Strike Eagle and served as the assistant chief of standardization and evaluation.

ron and suggested we fly together "before the whole thing was over." It would be fun to later tell our mutual friends that we had flown in the war together. By now I felt I could get a legal night's sleep so I ask the schedulers to put us on for the next evening. Sometime after midnight I drove back to the tent.

Saturday, January 19th

I woke mid morning, took a shower and ate some lunch before heading to the flightline. Against the schedule the munitions crews were finishing the loadout for the night's sorties. Then, around 1330, I got a call from the planning cell in Riyadh. Intelligence had located "the motherload" of scud sites, and General Glosson had changed our targets. I immediately called Ray* and asked him to bring his guys for a meeting at the 336th. His approach to the change, as always, was not why but "how fast." As the aircrews tried to get detailed targeting information, the maintenance guys did the impossible—they downloaded the conventional ordinance from twenty-four fighters and uploaded cluster munitions.

The flight brief was wrought with professional passion. We did not have the targeting data we needed to accurately plan our attack, nor would Riyadh send us any imagery. Not until we were leaving the squadron did any more precise information arrive.

Sergeant "Rock'in Rodney" Williams greeted me in the life support tent where we kept our flight gear. While I zipped

* Colonel Ray Davies was the Deputy Commander for Maintenance (MA). Traditionally, the DO and MA were at odds over flying versus fixing aircraft—not so with us. We trusted each other. Since day one at Thumrait we had worked the training schedule together, often on the back of an envelope at dinner.

on my g-suit and checked my helmet and oxygen mask, he offered his best wishes and insured I had the latest search and rescue gizmos. Then I headed out toward the ramp to walk to the jet with Grif. Rounding the squadron tent in the dark I bumped into Colonel Hal Hornburg, the wing commander and good friend. Originally we were both going to fly this night but then decided one of us should be on the ground. I said I'd fly tonight if he didn't mind. He agreed and now wished me "good luck." My reply: "This one's worth twenty years of flight pay."

CHAPTER 1

The End

Coming off the tanker, we headed North into Iraq—
twelve F-15Es. We were late for our times-on-targets, but
pushing it up, I saw we could make it. The importance of this
strike still echoed in my mind and I was not going to call it off.
We had to do this; we had to press on! Our targets: SCUD
missiles and chemical weapons storage sites at Al Qaim near
the influx of the Euphrates River.

Approaching the target area at 21,000 feet and 580
knots, we became aware that surface-to-air radars were locked
onto our aircraft. Unlike the first night of the war when we
ingressed at very low altitude, tonight the Iraqi radar could see
us coming. The numerous red threat circles briefed by our
intelligence officers had come alive. For a split second I thought
of the gunfight scene at the OK Corral.

Turning right at nine miles on a final heading to the
target, I looked down to the right and saw what could have
been an oil well fire blazing below us in the void of the black
desert. Training told me otherwise; it was the red-orange burner
plume of a SAM (surface-to-air missile) closing on us.

As it came closer, I pulled the aircraft right to force the
missile to overshoot and then rolled back left to get the target

symbol onto the heads-up display. Rolling out to wings level, a brilliant white light consumed us from the left front. Its blinding force seemed to paralyze our souls. Instinctively, I knew, "We're hit!"

Something was different in the cockpit. My eyes were drawn to the firelights on the left side of the instrument panel; I struggled to focus. Almost serendipitously, I realized we were still alive, but we had to get out immediately. Subconsciously, I was already reacting; instinctively my hands were reaching to grip the ejection levers to the sides of my seat—there had been no fumbling around—I could feel the friction of the metal-on-metal as I raised and squeezed the levers.

CHAPTER 2

Evasion in the Desert

My mind's eye was fixed on an orange glow on the horizon. I felt nothing, not my arms or legs or even my heart beating. I wasn't aware I was even breathing. In the deadly silence of the desert, I thought I was dreaming.

Where am I? In Oman? No, I'm in Saudi. I must be outside my tent. I must have stumbled while going to the toilet. This is not real, or is it? Had I been flying? Slowly, I began to remember. Yes, I had been flying. The war had started. I had been flying—a deep strike into the Northwest. But where am I now—back in Saudi? I must be dreaming. No, I must be in Iraq, but how did I get here?

I sensed I was kneeling upright. Then, my knee moved and I could feel the rocky surface and hear the grit of the loose shale. Although my head and body remained rigid, my vision began to expand. In the starlight, I could see my survival raft floating on the flat desert sea in front of me. Out to my left, my parachute was laid out where I had evidently disconnected it from my harness. Surprisingly, I was holding my run-away survival packet from my seat kit. A cold chill surged through my waking body. Slowly, I stood, staggered, and then instinctively retrieved my parachute and pulled the silk panels around my shoulders for warmth. Moving forward to my raft for some shelter from the cold wind, I realized I must be going into shock and reached for my water bottle from my lower right g-suit pocket. The cool drink helped me hold my consciousness. It was all too real. Alone with the silent stars, I became aware of the emptiness of my surroundings in the Iraqi desert.

The sound of a truck approaching snapped me into the fatality of the situation; I was now the game, not the hunter. A few yards away I could make out a concrete buttress supporting the base of a high voltage power line stanchion. I scrambled, half crawling, to hide behind it. Lying facedown, I dared to even breathe. The truck had come over a rise and made a slight turn to the left as it approached my landing area before stopping. It wasn't fifty yards away. Fortunately, the headlights had not crossed my raft or me. The engine stopped—I strained for the sounds of dogs or the shuffling of soldiers unloading.

One man got out and stood motionless beside the old pickup. He was apparently alone. I heard the scratch of a match and then saw a burst of flame. The red glow of his cigarette seemed to light up the sky like an eerie beacon of danger. My heart was pounding so hard I knew it must be echoing across the desert floor; I gasped for air. Finally, he finished his smoke, got back in the truck and, turning away, miraculously drove off the same way he had come.

Now, fully conscious of my survival situation, I knew it was critical to get away from my landing area. The only escape references I had were the orange glow, which I assumed to be our planned target area and the power lines overhead. Since we were hit before the target, I must be generally South of Al Qaim. Therefore, if I could keep moving under the lines, I would have a steady direction to clear the area and their straight-line path would keep me from wandering in a circle in the dark.

With my parachute draped over my shoulder like some old barnstormer who had just wrecked his bi-wing in a corn-field in Kansas, I headed out into the dark and unknown. As I began to walk slowly, I visualized my wingman and the other F-15Es high above, heading south without me. The loneli-ness sank in. I was several hundred miles north of the border in enemy territory—far from the comfort and camaraderie of the base and thousands of miles from my family at home at Seymour Johnson AFB in North Carolina and from my home-town of Brazil, Indiana. Oh, to be flying back to the base as we did the first night to the cheers and salutes of the crew chiefs. I recalled my ironic comments to waiting press mem-bers as "Two Dogs" McIntyre and I walked across the ramp to maintenance debrief, "I think it's been a good start." But now, I was here, alone, in the middle of nowhere, and who even knew? The vast expanse of the sky, the silence, the emp-tiness seemed to bury my consciousness in the shuffling sound of my unsteady steps.

Staring up at the stars, my thoughts were suddenly flooded with the words of the Twenty-third psalm:

Yea, though I walk through the valley of the shadow of death, I will fear no evil. . .For I am with thee.

Again and again, those words resonated through my mind; my confidence surged. I knew I was not alone. My shepherd was on guard.

As I continued, I thought of Barbara and Timm and of the distance that now separated us. I wondered how we would ever get back together. If only they could see that I was okay, that I was making my way south, walking in the desert. There were no lights, only the canopy of stars. Just as the night had been our protection in combat, the darkness now gave me the cover to put some distance between the crash site and me. My eyes adjusted to the darkness and I walked more confidently, almost boldly in the dark. In my mind the encouragement of the psalm, *the Lord is my shepherd, I shall not want.*

I thought of Fleenor, Borling, and Fant *—guys I had known who had spent a lifetime in the prisons of Vietnam. They made it home, so would I. For now, I'm here. Only God knows why…there must be a reason.

I knew I needed to broadcast on my survival radio but I was afraid to highlight my position or situation to the Iraqis. I had just evaded what might have been their only search effort. Maybe they thought I went down with the plane. Still, I should attempt to contact the AWACS; I had to try.

"Mayday, Mayday, this is Corvette Three on guard. This is Corvette Three in the blind. How do you read?"

I waited, then tried again. "This is Corvette 03 on guard, how do you read?"

"Mayday, mayday! This is Corvette Zero Three, over." Silence. The only sound was my boots shuffling along on the sandy shale surface. It seemed there was nothing out here except small tumbleweed-like, dead scrub bushes. Then I saw it,

---

* Brig Gen (retired) Ken Fleenor and Anne had been friends since his return from Hanoi in 1973 and assignment as the wing commander at Randolph AFB Texas. They were among the first to call Barbara with words of optimism and support. Maj Gen (retired) John Borling, also a long-term Vietnam POW and my former Group Commander in Europe, provided empathic counsel on service issues and media relations.
Lieutenant Commander (retired) Bob Fant had been my seminar leader at staff college after returning from six years in Vietnam.

like a specter, sitting ominously upright in the moonlight—an ejection seat. Grif, I'd been flying with Grif. I remembered now. We had been flying together. I hadn't even thought about my backseater. Grif, oh my God. I didn't want to find him sitting there, dead, or badly injured. Closer, I could see the empty seat. Thank God he's not here.

Suddenly, headlights appeared in the distance to my right. I fell to the ground.

Another truck. This time on a road approximately a quarter mile away that appeared to parallel the power lines. It was a large troop transport vehicle moving south to north at moderate speed and seemingly not coming after me. I had to keep moving.

Cautiously, I made another radio call in the blind. This time there was an answer: "Three Alpha, this is Bravo."

"Grif, where are you?" I said. And then quickly realized the foolishness of my question. Here we are in the middle of nowhere in the pitch black of night and I ask him where he is and expect him to say something like, "Over here on the porch of the pro shop."

Just then, the lights of another truck appeared coming up the road. "Grif, can you see the truck?"

"Yes," he replied.

"Can you see the big power line?" I whispered.

"Yes."

"I'm under the power line. I'll give you a hack when the truck is abeam my position."

Soon, I heard someone coming toward me in the brush. And then, my old friend came walking out of the dark.

I can't even remember if we embraced. I do remember that we hardly spoke. There was a quiet acceptance of the seriousness of the situation and a mutual understanding of the urgency to keep going, to get as much distance as possible from the crash site and to find a place to hide before light. The darkness was providing cover that would be gone in the morning.

Whether from exhaustion or because we couldn't find a better place, we finally collapsed by some scrub brush on the bank of a shallow wadi. We both took a drink of water and then, huddled together and wrapped in my parachute, we fell asleep.

Back Home

Some time after 8 p.m. the command post at Seymour Johnson received an official casualty notification message from the Air Force Personnel Center and executed the key staff recall. Colonel "Jumbo" Wray hurriedly met with the assembled team that included our friend Chaplain Steward Smith and then drove home to join Nancy, his wife, before walking across the street to our home on base. Meanwhile, a duplicate team headed into town to knock on the door where Liz Griffith was home with their four children.

Normally it is customary for the team to wear uniforms, but in this case since it was Saturday night, "Jumbo" rightfully felt it was more appropriate to go in civilian clothes. He also directed the team to wait out of sight near our home to avoid the dreaded *blue-car-in-the-driveway* horror for Barbara.

At approximately 10 p.m. they knocked on the carport door. Inside, Barbara and Ann had finished Chinese carryout and were about to play a video I had made of a typical day for me in Oman.

While it was not unusual for Jumbo and Nancy to stop

over unannounced, it was unusual for Jumbo to walk in first, in front of Nancy. Barbara was suspicious and looked cautiously out the door toward the street. "Well, I guess it's okay," she said. "There's no one in the driveway." Half-smiling, she nervously turned around and then realized the look in their eyes. "Barbara, we need to talk," he said. Softly, he put his comforting arms around her. As they moved into the living room, the official team, including Cynthia Hornburg and Carol Rathje came in the front door.

Barbara called Uncle Ed and simply said, "It's time" and asked that someone call our close friends in town, Nancy and Frank Newkirk and Cheryl and Dick Hoey. As she recalls, they arrived shortly and joined the others in the living room. Both Nancy and Cheryl were prepared to stay with Barbara.

In the midst of all the emotion, Timm returned with his girlfriend and had been sitting in the driveway. He found it curious that all these people had been coming into the house and finally went inside through the carport door to the kitchen. He was engulfed by speechless stares as Barbara, who had returned to the kitchen, quickly moved forward. "It will be all right," she said as she wrapped him in her mothering arms. Once again Jumbo ebbed the tide with comforting words.

Around midnight, after calling several friends across the country to put me on their prayer chain, Barbara asked Chaplain Smith to open the base chapel and invited our friends to join her and Timm. The small group gathered at the altar and offered prayers for our safe return. Privately she feared the torture we had associated with those captured and held so long in Vietnam. Would sudden death have saved him from such pain? She wondered. It seemed such a macabre contradiction of emotions. Following the informal gathering, as Timm and the chaplain walked slowly down the aisle to join the others in the narthex, Steward asked him how he felt about my situation. Timm replied, "I know he's okay, I can see him walking in the desert."

In Brazil, Indiana, it was around midnight when Lt Col Ted Wright from the Air Force ROTC office at Indiana State University and a deputy sheriff knocked on the door to awaken my mother, Evelyn, and stepfather, Bill Wallace. Although his manner was consoling, the Pentagon message was brief: "...no chutes were sighted and no radio contact was received."

There was little emotion there in the living room. "I knew what it was when I saw the deputy and the other men," Bill said. "I was very calm when they delivered the message," recalled my Mother. "I knew it might come since they are in such a precarious position over there. It was just a statement that I would have to accept," quoted the *Brazil Daily Times*. A very strong believer, she too put her trust in the Lord. "We just have to believe that God's watching over him. I feel like he is alive...I feel I can see him walking around in a foreign country."

Sunday, January 20th—the first day.

I remember stirring from the chill of the morning air and opening my eyes to the vast nothingness that spread around us. It was overcast, cold and damp. I could see my breath. Nothing had changed except now we could see the Iraqi desert surrounding us.

"Holy shit! You've got an ugly hole in the back of your head," Grif blurted. "You're soaked in blood."

Then he unzipped his survival vest to get some dressing stuff to stop the bleeding. As he applied pressure, he asked if it hurt. I hadn't felt any pain, but sure enough, I was soaked. From the waist up, my dark green flightsuit was now a dark brown. What I had thought was sweat running down my back was blood. Then, from the distance, the sound of another heavy truck made us realize the frailty of our current hiding place. There was no time for first aid. And besides, I really didn't think I was hurt that badly.

Now we could see the road—a two-lane highway that indeed paralleled the high voltage lines. While it served as a good reference, we needed to get farther away from the truck traffic. In the distance was a hill—a couple of hundred yards in front of us. Everything else was flat desert with patches of scrub brush. Our best hope for a hiding place was atop the hill, but making the trek would be risky in the daylight. We would have to crawl to avoid being seen from the road.

Staring at the hill we suddenly realized that the visibility was quickly going down. It was getting foggy! We watched in awe as our refuge was disappearing in a cloud. The blanket of fog was rapidly moving in our direction and soon covered the road. This was our queue. Time to go.

Together we tried to run, but instead found ourselves stumbling, out of breath, and tripping on scrub as we supported each other to make our way to the hill. Approaching the base, we could see the fog was clearing just as fast as it had come. Grif and I hurriedly crawled up a sort of goat trail some fifty feet through the rocks. As the road came into view, we rolled into a shallow stony depression on top. This would have to do.

Considering the alternatives as we gazed across the

moonscape of our surroundings, the hilltop would at least give us some protection and a vantagepoint to the road. It was almost like our cockpit—a catbird seat that gave us a false sense of security. Instead of soaring, we were now eagles pinned in a nest. We couldn't stand but there was enough side-stone cover to sit up or crawl around. Best of all, the rocks absorbed the sun's heat to soothe our aching bodies and warm our backs at night. Again, I don't remember any "woe is me" conversation or even any exchange on what happened. Our lives had so changed in an instant of time. How tenderly wrought is our destiny: some things are far beyond our wildest imagination—others just happen.

At this point it didn't matter how we got there or even why. We were in enemy territory and evading for our lives. All our resources, all our energy, all our focus must be on surviving. We did agree: "If we can just stay alive, we will eventually get home." As I lay there staring at the sky, my thoughts lost in the expanse of our surroundings, I remembered the story of the mustard seed. God knows where we are. He's right here, watching over us.

Exhausted from the trek, I must have dozed off in the warm sun. The distant sound of voices and the pain of the a sharp rock in my back brought me back to reality. Quickly I rolled over and crawled up to look over the rocks toward the road. On the highway, I saw two trucks pulled off on our side—the northbound lane. Two men were talking and walking around a trailer truck cab. Then they got into the truck, turned around and drove south leaving the first truck parked near a drainage conduit. My mind was filled with intrigue: could this be some sort of rescue rendezvous or was this a setup by the Iraqis to flush us out?

Besides the activity on the road, we were concerned with our blind sides to the east and south. We could easily watch our most active threat along the highway to the west, but lookouts to the east and south required exposing ourselves above the rimline. Out of fear of interception, we maintained our radio vigilance in a listen-only mode and only used one radio to conserved battery power. I guess the scenes from too many James Bond movies provided the visuals for an enemy helicopter to pop up on our east side and blow us away. For now, all was quiet and the best we could do was stay put and stay focused. We knew where we were; we just needed to be patient and sort out a plan.

Together we had about two pints of water, no food, one parachute canopy with cords, one solar blanket, our survival vests plus parts of one seat kit, and our .38 revolvers. In our vests we had an old model survival radio, some pen flares, a compass, a small first aid kit, our pointy-talky blood chits and an area escape and evasion map.

Late afternoon we heard the sound of friendly fighters overhead. Immediately, we called: "This is Corvette Three on guard, this is Corvette Three on guard, how do you read?" Three times we called, hoping for any acknowledgment. Nothing.

That night, we heard the sounds of fighters again. This time, the distinct sound of F-15s high above. They were going back (to our targets).

Grif quickly broadcast into the darkness: "Allied aircraft in the wadi area, this is Corvette Zero-Three." Tonight a familiar voice responded. It was Gary Cole from the Rocket Squadron.

"Corvette Zero-Three, this is Chevy Zero Six. We read

you loud and clear."

And then, "Hang tight...they're searching."

"Get on with it," I interrupted. "Tell them to hurry up."

And then there was silence. The sound of the engines faded into the darkness leaving us alone with the silent stars and the emptiness of our misfortune. Nothing more was said. We just moved closer together to keep warm, pulled the parachute over our heads, and wearily fell asleep.

Day 2, Monday.

The road activity and the mystery of the parked truck kept me mentally engaged while Grif monitored the radio through an earpiece. Food and water were starting to be a concern. Especially water. We had ventured a peek to the northeast and saw what looked like a ranch. Again, daydreams of James Bond schemes to search the house were discounted by concerns for detection and having to deal with civilians. Likewise, we had ruled out going back to retrieve additional water from our ejection seat survival kits. Right or wrong, we didn't feel it was worth the risk.

The one plan we were considering was to hijack a car along the road. We figured we could work our way down through the wadi to the culvert and then wait. One of us would either lie on the edge of the road or cautiously hail a passing car. When the car stoppped, the other guy would come up from behind the driver with his pistol drawn. The problem with this scenario was again the possibility of killing a civilian(s). Then what? If we demanded he take us to the border, we considered the risk of such a high visibility crossing at a Checkpoint Charlie-type military guard post. Crashing through a border post seemed to be a low probability option of surviving. Confounding all these options was the second appearance by another man at the abandoned truck. What if he had put food and water and some note in the cab?

Suddenly, the radio came alive. Rescue forces were engaged with Slate 46 *. Activity was feverous. Our response was immediate. "Break, break. This is Corvette Three on guard, how do you read?" Again and again on both radios, we tried to break in. Still no response—and then silence. We just couldn't make radio contact with anyone.

I had always felt we were too far north to be rescued. Saturday night's strike mission had been deeper than any other friendly forces had gone and, in my mind, it would take too long for a rescue team to come so far in-country from the Saudi border. Now, unsuccessful in breaking in to the Slate 46 rescue on the radio, I was convinced we were on our own and that it was time to move. We agreed our only hope was to walk out through Syria.

The night before we had seen the lights of two towns in the distance. One, Abu Kamal looked to be about ten miles away in Syria. The border could be as close as eight miles in a straight line. Our map showed a parallel north-south road about a mile past the border leading to the towns, and there were two hills lying along the south side of our proposed route that could help us navigate in the dark. Somewhere in the first town we thought we could get help.

Late afternoon we began to prepare for our escape to

* SLATE 46 (US Navy F-14). LT Devon Jones and LT Larry Slade were shot down in the early morning hours of January 21st. The SAR effort was approximately 40 km southeast of our location. LT Jones was rescued; LT Slade was captured.

Syria. We cut the metal hardware and the cord lines off the parachute canopy and then fashioned the dark panel sections into flowing headdresses and robes to mute our silhouettes. Camo cream from our survival kit further darkened our faces. The extra white silk sections were stuffed inside our flightsuits for insulation from the cold. We piled rocks on the stuff we decided not to take and then anxiously waited for dusk.

CHAPTER 3

Escape to Syria

The trials of our journey were masked by the tranquillity of the pastel contrail left by the big orange sun as it fell below the Iraq-Syrian horizon on its way to Goldsboro. Here, it was symbolically High Noon—time to head-out.

I was intently focused on the abandoned truck that had consumed my imagination for the past two days. We had to move before it got too dark to check it out. As we cautiously came off the hill there was no looking back. All our senses were alert for any sound or sight of the enemy. In the twilight we made our way across the several hundred yards of sand and scrub to the road. Grif correctly moved toward the culvert; I toward the truck. It was nothing but a scorched, burned-out hulk. No food, no water, no cryptic note. Now, no more time to waste.

Grif crawled through the conduit; I brazenly continued over the road. Our focus was now on the 210-foot elevation ridge of the first of two hills we planned to pass to the north of on our westerly track. We were now over a week from the new moon, and the rising quarter moon seemed like a spotlight on the sandy desert scape. On the horizon, off-line to the right, we could see the lights of Abu Kamal. Overhead, an angel began to light the stars.

In the cover of darkness, we walked upright. It felt good to be on the move, our spirits were high. We talked softly about what we might do when we got to the town; I know we both continued to pray. My thoughts dwelled momentarily on the Easter hymn lyrics, *He walks with me and talks with me,* and then returned to the village.

I imagined a rural, almost western-type setting with a dirt street, a raised wooden sidewalk, and a phone booth near the corner of a building on the main street. Remembering the story of the National Guard soldier who called the States during the Granada invasion, I felt we could call the Seymour Johnson command post and tell Colonel "Jumbo" Wray, the acting commander and my neighbor, where we were. I knew he could get it done when it came to making the right calls. Besides, I knew my AT&T phone card number and figured it would be easier to call the US than Riyadh or Al Kharj.

We also talked about whether to try to contact the local police. Our pointy-talky blood chits would help with the language problem although this close to the border there could be sympathy toward Iraq. And besides, we might be worth a big bounty.

Still, with hopes high, it was easy to imagine that we were on our way home and back to flying. Maybe we would have to fly commercially out of Damascus. I hoped we would not have to go by way of the States; we needed to get to Al Kharj. No doubt the flight doc would probably make us rest a few days, but then we needed to get back in the air (if the war wasn't over). All we needed was a good shower and a couple hot meals. I felt great. *Thank you, God, for showing us the way out of Iraq.*

Sometime after passing abeam the peak of the first ridge, we heard the sound of barking dogs in the distance. My first thought was, who would have a kennel out here? Then I shuddered to think it might be a pack of wild dogs or even military search dogs. Still, we continued on, keeping our bearing in relation to the lights to our right front quarter and to the hills off our left.

The barking grew louder. Suddenly, from out of the darkness, they were upon us—a pack of eight to twelve big shepherd-type dogs. They had surrounded me, probably attracted by the smell of dried blood from my neck injury. This was no welcome party. A couple of the larger ones were lunging and seemed to be sizing me for the take down. I gathered my robe so as not to give them something to bite nor could I afford to trip into their prey. Cautiously, we kept walking. I had my arms pulled up to my chest with my right hand on the revolver holstered in my survival vest on my left side.

The lead dog had taken up a position inches off my right front side. His white teeth glistened in the moonlight; his eyes glowed like the devil. I felt that any second he would go for my leg. "It's okay," I whispered, as if he understood English. "It's okay." Then, drawing and cocking my gun, I realized that he was so close I couldn't even extend my arm to point at him without touching his head. For Grif several yards away it was an impossible shot in the dark. Plus, a gunshot would echo across the desert and attract unwanted attention. Afraid I might stumble on a rock and inadvertently squeeze the trigger, I released the hammer on my gun and said another prayer. *Lord, this is not the way it should end.* I thought again of the valley of the shadow of death. *Protect us Lord, for thine is the power and glory forever.*

In the shadows, we could now make out the shapes of two large tents. We had come upon a Bedouin camp. My mind's eye saw a figure standing outside one of the tents holding a traditional long rifle. Firing on his dogs would be a big mistake. This was not a bed and breakfast hospitality stop. We had to just keep moving.

Slowly we made our way beyond the camp. Before they withdrew, the dogs seemed to be scolding us for trespassing.

Walking on, our trek became easier—fewer rocks and no scrub. We could see in the moonlight that we were on some sort of dirt road. It was not paved with yellow bricks but as long as it was going our way, okay. After all, it was night, we were in the middle of the desert and except for the Bedouin camp we passed, we couldn't imagine anyone else was out here. And, like our time on the hill, we expected to see the lights of any traffic a great distance across the flat terrain.

Suddenly, like a hippo at a theme park, a large WWII style diesel truck came flying up out of nowhere in front of us. Face-on and close enough to see the bars in the grille, we dove for the side of the road as the truck roared by.

Unbelievable! How could they not have seen us?

Maybe our disguises had worked; maybe they thought we were just wandering desert Bedouins.

Hearts pounding, we pressed on—off the road, which now veered from our course. It was evident we had to pay more attention; these mistakes could get us killed.

The waist-high tumbleweed we now encountered slowed our progress, yet the lights of the town were getting closer and we could infrequently see headlights on the distant across-border road. Under the quarter moon, we could also make out a large north-south wadi and on the far side, two small hills that looked like camel humps. On the right side, there appeared to be a cabin or shed-type structure.

Moving on, we worked our way farther to the right to avoid being seen if there was anyone near the building. It would be easy to alter our course toward the Syrian town although our priority was to cross the border at the closest point.

By sometime around midnight or later, we had gotten through the wadi and then around the right side of the hill to a point that was a couple hundred yards beyond the shed. We estimated we were now less than a kilometer from the border with plenty of darkness left to finish the journey before daylight. We had been walking since sundown and needed to rest.

The sky had completely cleared; the stars added their light to the serene scape and the wind now stirred, wicking away the sweat from our face and neck. It had been quite a hike. Considering we hadn't eaten in three days and had had little water, we were exhausted.

Sitting there in the scrub, we shared the last swallows of our water. Then, surprisingly, through our radio earpieces a call came over the survival net.

"Corvette 03, Mobil 51."

Almost daring to respond, we replied: "Mobil 51, this is Corvette 3, go ahead."

He asked for our condition and our location. Grif replied that we were "together and OK," then quickly gave our location in relation to our fragged target.

All we heard was "Standby."

Where had everybody been? I wondered. Here we were on the border of Syria seemingly perched to escape after evading the Iraqis for three nights and now somebody checks in on the radio! If these were rescue forces, we really had no choice but to wait. Dutifully, we readied our pen flares and listened.

The wind chilled our souls and we huddled even closer together. Physically, we were not in good shape and our hope now hung on the anticipation of the next radio call.

Silence. Not even a crackle on the air.

With growing frustration, we broke our radio silence and called: "Mobil 51, this is Corvette 3, over." Then impatiently, again: "Mobil 51, this is Corvette 3. How do you read?"

Nothing.

Frustrated by the anxiety of our situation, we began to question the phantom sound of a helicopter in the wind and the illogical sight of a red light in the distance to the east. We were now captured by our own inability to continue on with our plan for what had seemed the right way out. Under the clear sky, we shivered in the cold. The logic of "riding out" versus facing the unknown across the border in Syria prevailed. It was my flawed decision to at least get relief near the shed from the piercing wind. I had lost caution of any previous activity there and thought it was abandoned. Besides, we had no idea how much longer it would be before we would be picked up by the Mobil 51* rescue team.

I started back. Grif was about ten steps off my left and trailing. As I cautiously approached the small building I saw a window and then saw the faint flickering of a candle. A nervous chill penetrated my cold body; I froze. Then, like the Pink Panther cartoon character, I tried to step back. Within a

---

* Mobil 51 was in reality an F-15C on a high-altitude combat air patrol sortie. After making initial contact, he was directed to "get off Guard (channel)," and he made no further attempt to contact us.

few steps the building seemed to erupt. One voice, then gun-fire. Automatic weapons fire came from on top and both sides. It was like being in the middle of a firecracker display at a Fourth of July celebration; the difference tonight was the ominous loss of our freedom.

CHAPTER 4

Saddam

"Iraq, Syria! Iraq, Syria! Iraq, Syria!" they yelled as they continued to fire.

The muzzle fires were almost blinding, like the wall of sparklers when you stand too close to the fireworks display on the 4th of July. I dared not move or breathe. It was no time to flinch let alone turn to run just to be shot in the back. I could see the sand being kicked up as the bullets ricocheted around me; my ears rang with the sound of passing shot; I was in awe that I felt no pain. Surely, I thought, I must be hit.

"English, English!" I began to shout in response and then cautiously allowed myself to lower to my knees with my palms forward. To my left, slightly back, Grif too, had seemly survived the barrage. If we had already crossed into Syria, it was closer than expected.

Now, cautiously, they came forward. I felt like that snared pesky rabbit looking up the barrel of Farmer Jones' shotgun, thinking at any moment my head would be blown off. They grabbed me by the upper arms and half dragged me around the corner of the building to the door. Just inside, I felt the warmth of the shelter once sought but now regretted. Quickly, we were pushed through another door and into a small room. As we stumbled ahead, I caught a glimpse of a large portrait of a man with a mustache on the wall to the right. There were a couple of chairs, maybe a bench but most importantly there was a pot-bellied heater in front of us. Up to my left hung that haunting picture. In the chaos of the moment my mind finally made the match. There was no doubt, it was Saddam. We didn't make it.

CHAPTER 5

The Sort

Who could have imagined that in the middle of the night somewhere along the Northwestern Iraqi border with Syria, two American aviators would approach a seemly deserted guard post shack where they sought shelter from the cold while awaiting an apparent inbound rescue force. Not the Iraqis.

The chaos of the moment helped hide my inner reaction to the identity of the man with the mustache. Now, sitting side-by-side on a cot ironically covered with an old US Army blanket, we were playing out our roles as neither side could have ever imagined. Here, far from the headquarters in Baghdad or the front in Basrah, two strangers had suddenly triggered unprecedented excitement. Our dark green silk parachute robes and headscarves, dirty faces, and famished stares served only to confound the inevitable start of that old television game show, "What's My Line?"

Leaning into the stove, I tried to cover my survival vest. "Water. Water, please," I asked, continuing to shiver. One soldier offered water, another hot tea. "Thank you... danke...gracious," I mumbled in gratitude.

Noticing the blood on my face and neck, another man reached into the corner and picked up a dark colored bottle with cotton stuffed in the top. He shook it once and then used the stuffing to dab my wounds with some yellowish liquid.

"Who are you?" began the leader in broken English.

"Where do you come from?"

"How did you come here?"

Slowly, portending confusion, I replied. "From the east. We've been in the desert, walking for three days."

"No!" replied one. "The wolves. You would have been eaten by the wolves."

"You are English!"

"Ameriki?"

"English, yes," I said.

"You are Ameriki!"

"Yes, we are from United States."

"Please, food, eat. More tea." I pleaded, trying to hide our identity.

Now, they started to search us. Without the robes, our vests and flightsuits became apparent. Worst of all, they saw our guns. The gig was up. The bandits were sorted and we were identified as the enemy.

Our vest and g-suit pockets became the immediate focus of intense interest. All I had in my pockets was my flightline security badge and a $10 bill. The flares, our survival radios, and our escape and evasion kits were like new Christmas toys. One guy nearly fired off one of our pen gun flares. As another fumbled with the radio, I took it back and tried to palm the batteries as I expressed frustration and pretended to move a switch.

The guy-in-charge unfolded our survival map and then begin to read the pointy-talky barter chit. The American flag got little respect but the paragraph on a reward brought about some discussion.

"What this mean? he asked.

"If you will let us go on. . .if you will take us across the border, we can get you a lot of money."

"How much?" he inquired skeptically.

"500,000 dollars. Really," I said. "Our government will pay you. We can go just across the border to Syria...we can get you all this money."

Blank stares. We were getting nowhere. The guy-in-charge made a call on an old crank field phone and abruptly regained his bearings. Slamming down the phone, he barks an order; two others hastily tie our hands and they stuff our belongings into a gunnysack.

It was time to go.

There were just too many of them for one guy to be coerced to help. Besides, Saddam had evidently put out some sort of bounty on downed coalition airmen.* No, our only chance was to get out of here alive and look for an escape opportunity later, or try to cut a deal with the next guys. This was not simply like being captured in a child's game of blind man's bluff. We were playing for our lives.

---

* Saddam had placed a bounty of $90,000 on any captured pilot.

CHAPTER 6

The Pitch

"Ameriki!" cursed the soldier as he spit in my face.

The outside was even colder now without the silk parachute stuffing in our flight suits. Our hands were tied with heavy rope and our path was now a gantlet of unfettered barbarians. Punching and pushing, they half threw us into the back of a pickup truck and then kicked us toward the cab. One guard with a machine gun sat by the tailgate. Only a few dirty gunnysacks cushioned our ride as we bounced along in the dark. No sympathy here, nor could we imagine the nightmare ahead.

The truck stopped at another shack. Inside, there was a soldier, maybe an officer, sitting at a desk in a room off to the right. He spoke a little better English and so we started over: ". . .three days in the desert, no food, no water."

He offered us something hot to drink and a hard-boiled egg.

"Yes, we were United States."

"No, we did not bomb. We were just flying and had an airplane problem."

"Can you help us. . .going to Syria."

"This (pointy-talky) means that if you will let us go on

. . .if you will just help us get to the border. . .we can get you a lot of money. 500,000 dollars. Our government will pay you."

And so the conversation went on. Since there was only one other guy in the room it seemed like we might have a chance. But, he couldn't be bought either.

Suddenly the talking was over. We were back in the truck with only a slight hope that we were headed west.

CHAPTER 7

Al Qaim

The large security gate at the compound screeched as it opened. It was late; the place seemed deserted. The driver pulled forward a couple hundred yards and then stopped at a ranch style building like an old Caphardt-era military base house with a white Chevy Caprice in a carport to the left side. After some animated talking at the side door, the soldier took us inside. By now it must have been two to three o'clock in the morning (Tuesday, January 22).

The partially paneled room was large—a combination living room and office. To my right was a television, straight ahead a couch. The back wall was a large built-in bookcase with a desk and conference table. Two other doors opened into the room from the other side.

In a few minutes a man in pajamas came into the room from the left door. My first instinct was to ask if we could turn on the television to see how the war was going. Fortunately, I caught myself, recognizing we were cheering for different teams.

Considering the hour, the conversation was not too probing; we could hardly be expected to be coherent anyway. If this was a courtesy call, I guess we survived. He didn't order us to be shot—at least not immediately. Within minutes we were taken outside and around the corner to a bunkhouse type building where we were chained to steel cots. The good news was that there was a heater between us and another one of those US Army blankets on the mattress. Once secured to the cots, we were left alone. The door was locked and the guards posted outside. Grif and I briefly coordinated our stories on aircraft capabilities and agreed escape seemed improbable in our current physical state. For the first time in days I took off my boots and rolled over on my side. I remember starting to say the Lord's Prayer, but I must have fallen asleep immediately.

It was already light when the sound of the key in the lock on the door woke me. A new chill penetrated my body—this was no dream.

The soldiers indicated we were in their room and turned up the heater. As I sat up and extended my feet, I decided to take off my socks to put them on the heater. Seeing my ankles for the first time since the ejection explained why they had seemed weak. They both were ugly black and blue from when I hit the ground in my parachute. I guess my tight-laced boots had kept them from swelling and given me support.

"Damn," I had foolishly just let my socks burn on the heater. The soldiers laughed and then most surprisingly one of them got me a pair of his—brown with red Polo insignia. I still put my burned socks on over his for warmth and tightly laced up my boots as they signaled it was time to go.

We were led back inside the commander's quarters. Now there were three or four older men in uniform sitting around the table. It was hardly a time for cordial introductions. Grif and I may have sat momentarily but were then taken into a back room and then individually brought out for questioning.

It seemed these guys were the unit commanders under this area commander. Their primary interest was air defense. They wanted to know what could they do to better protect themselves and more pointedly, what were the attackers' vulnerabilities?

They found my explanation hard to believe. We were flying "a new airplane that was not yet equipped with self protection systems." Surely "the political pressure to get as many airplanes to the gulf" must have been tremendous if "we were ordered to bring these new bombers over just last week before they were ready for combat" and then "we flew them without support aircraft" thinking "the darkness would protect us." If these planes were so new it seemed likely "we had electrical problems." No wonder we crashed, they must have thought.

The story seemed to hold—at least for now.

While Grif was being questioned, I was in the right-front side room being watched by a unarmed guy in his early twenties. There was no exterior door off this area but out the window I could see a small cluttered yard with a bicycle leaning against the side of the house and other adjacent buildings. After we talked awhile I asked to go to the bathroom thinking I might get a better look at the outside grounds and options for escape in case we were kept here. I didn't get far. The toilet area was just behind a curtain.

The kid was not upset nor did he seem to care that Grif and I might have been the ones to blow up part of his world. He could tell I was starved and I was eager to finish every glass of water he poured. Since it was approaching noon, he offered me some dates and then opened a can of sardines. The dates were great and I ate all the crackers I thought I could. As for the sardines, I wasn't dying yet!

After some time, I was recalled to the front room.

"You're lying!" came the charge from the commander. The discussion was over. We were blindfolded and handcuffed again and taken outside where we were put in the back seat of a white Toyota wagon. I was by the right window; Grif was in the middle with a guard on the left. In the front, a driver and another guard. Both appeared to be unarmed. Maybe this would be our chance to escape.

No sooner had we left the compound than they jerked off our blindfolds. What we saw was unbelievable. There in front of us was an army truck leading us down a wide dirt street toward a crowd of people on the edge of a village. The truck slowed and began to blow its horn to clear the peasants to the street sides. This was no casual weekday street scene in rural Iraq; these folks were fired up. I hit the plunger door lock and motioned to Grif. Instead of leaping to freedom, we needed to hope and pray we could get through this parade alive.

The crowd grew and the chanting grew louder and more agitated. Among other epitaphs, they were clearly chanting, "Saddam, Saddam! Saddam, Saddam!" Some near the front waved flags; others flailed sticks. This was not a hero's welcome, and we were not here for a key to the city.

Moving very slowly along for half a mile, we made a wide left U-turn and started back up the other side of the road. In the turn our car got farther behind the truck giving the growing crowd an opportunity to close in front of us. It was getting nasty and as I glanced at the driver, I could see he too was scared. Now stopped, we were surrounded. The jeering mob started rocking the car. Suddenly, the sound of breaking glass—a large grapefruit-sized rock came through the window behind me. This was "the valley of the shadow of death" and I prayed—*I will fear not, for thou are with us.*

"Get going!" I yelled. "Go!"

Nearly terrorized, the driver tried to accelerate through the wall of screaming peasants. With God's help, they moved, although I thought we must have rolled over some. The car gained speed and slowly cleared the crowd. Ahead, the gates of the compound looked mighty good. Whatever lay ahead, it seemed better than being beaten to death in Al Qaim.

CHAPTER 8

The Road to Baghdad

I'm not sure why we went back to the compound—maybe the shattered car window, maybe the driver's shorts. Anyway, once in the commander's driveway, we were taken out of the car and stood guarded in the yard near a willow tree while they yelled at each other. Then they blindfolded us again and pushed us back inside another similar car. Somewhere in the yelling, I heard "Baghdad."

If the treatment was bad, the journey was only a precursor to our spiral into Dante's worse nightmare. Cramped together, there was no way to get comfortable with our hands cuffed. We did struggle enough to get our seat belts on and I was able to move my blindfold a little to see out the bottom. The driver and his buddies acted like they were going off to the beach for the weekend—laughing and apparently telling jokes. As for the radio music, a torturous cross between hard rock and Arab bazaar, it was just too loud.

Shortly after night fall, half hoping for a stop at McDonalds or Burger King, we pulled off the highway to the right into a large complex of one-story white buildings similar to one of these u-rent-it places. The guy riding shotgun got out and beat on the door then we all went up a couple steps and filed inside. It must have been a rug merchant warehouse or outlet as there were oriental rugs hanging all around.

For our driver and the others it was old home week. Seemingly they blah, blah, blah'd about us and then dumped our stuff from the gunnysack on the floor. I was tired of telling the story and asked to "go to the toilet." After several days of dehydrating I finally did need to urinate and I wanted to see if there were any other guys being held here.

One guy led me outside and then around the corner down a muddy one-car dirt alleyway between two buildings. Even in the dark it was dismal; the kind of place where no one would ever find you. I kept talking to him, hoping if somebody heard my English, they might call out. Nothing. This can't be the place, we can't stay here, I told myself. Then my guard opened a door—I took one step in and pissed into the darkness.

When we got back, it was time to move on. They all beat each other on the back, smacked us on the back of the head and we were off—loud music and all. The only difference was now that we were approaching the city the driver didn't have his headlights on. How ironic, I thought. We had come this far and yet at any moment, we were going to die unceremoniously in a head-on car crash with these knuckleheads.

The city appeared deserted. The power was out and the streets were empty except for an infrequent on-coming car that flashed its parking lights. Unsure of where he was going, our driver continued to yell at the others. Finally, we turned left off the street, drove up a concrete ramp leading behind a large brick building and pulled up next to an entrance with large double glass doors. It was apparent that the place was empty but one guy got out and pounded on the door anyway. After a few minutes, our frustrated driver yelled at him to get back in the car and we sped off in the dark.

After speeding along city streets, we headed into a residential area. The neighborhood was even darker. Limbs and debris lay in the street as though a windstorm had added insult to the series of air attacks on the downtown. After a few lefts and rights, the driver turned left through a gate and pulled around left, parking in a courtyard area of a horseshoe-shaped one-story old brick building. This time someone came out to the car. The driver got out, and, in his usual riled and animated fashion, began to explain his cursed predicament—apparently what to do with us.

We were led inside a room off the left side of the courtyard into a small classroom with about five rows of bleacher seats. Grif and I sat side-by-side on the first level; our bag of stuff was thrown on the floor in front. Instead of a couple goons with machine guns, three teenage boys dressed in dark Nike nylon pants and tops were told to watch us.

These young men were well groomed, spoke good English, and were captivated by the opportunity to speak with two American pilots. As they rummaged through our stuff, we found out they were brothers aged eighteen to twenty and that the old man, their dad, was a retired soldier who now served as the commandant of this military school. They were anxious to talk about how it felt to fly the F-15; we were more interested in food. We asked for water or tea and told them briefly about our journey in the desert and that we hadn't eaten for almost four days. Abruptly one of the three left and then returned in a short time with some pieces of chicken and some dates.

This prompted a very valuable lesson in diplomatic courtesies:

"How do you say 'thank you' in Arabic?"

"SHOOK-ran," he replied.

"And 'water'?" I asked.

"MIA-ah."

"Thank you, SHOOK-ran."

The boys talked about how they wished to "go to America someday." Yet, as relaxed as the moment seemed, the boys realized we were the enemy and we were going nowhere—our armed guard was just outside the door. What we needed dreadfully now was a place to sleep. As we sat exhausted on the bench, I suggested that we could stay there with them. In response, one of the boys shook his head and then volunteered, "You'll have mattresses and blankets where you are going." With that, the old man and our driver showed up in the doorway.

"We go now."

CHAPTER 9

Are You Christmas?

We had lost all bearing as we zoomed along. Jumping from the car would be foolish. Besides, there was no way Grif could get out of the middle seat. We had to stay together and continue to keep our senses keen.

Coming off a boulevard and hooking back left, the driver turned right and parked the white Toyota wagon facing the main road on a side street. Out of the warm car, we were pushed along a narrow walkway bounded by tall evergreens that approached the small front porch from the right of the white clapboard house. The driver's knock on the door reflected his weariness and growing frustration; the agitated tone of the Arabic greeting from the man at the door signaled that we were not welcome and that this was just another stop to survive on our journey. Here, instead of another interrogation, however, we faced a most unusual opportunity: to witness to our faith and Christianity.

In the dim candlelight we saw the entry hall leading to a cross hallway with stairs on our right going up toward the front of the house to the second floor. Grif and I were made to sit side-by-side on the fourth row of steps. The doors to the other rooms were closed but we had gotten a glimpse of several men sitting around a heater in the room across from us. They were arguing loudly and it seemed as though they were cursing our driver for bringing us there. I sensed there were other people in the house and strained to hear any sounds or English voices indicating they might be holding other prisoners here. Maybe this was the place where we would be held.

We were guarded by two Iraqis; one had an automatic rifle, the other brandished a knife. One seemed more intent at jabbing at us and tormenting us in Arabic. At one point, he ripped Grif's T-shirt over his head and threatened us with his knife. This drew a rebuke from the other man and our agitator pulled back. Now we were alone with the armed guard standing at the foot of the stairs facing us. After some time, with the muffled talk in the background, he leaned forward and said quietly, "Are you Christmas?"

"Christmas?" I said, puzzled.

"He must mean Christian," Grif whispered.

Although my mind filled instantly with the fear that our Arab guard might simply be looking for a reason to kill us, I also felt that God was with us now as always. "Yes," I responded.

"Me, too," said the guard.

How ironic. Here, along this seemingly endless dismal road, we would meet a man with such courage.

And then it was time to go, again.

As we drove along, it was quiet. Our Iraqis had lost their joviality; we too had grown impatient and frustrated. I had lost interest in trying to remember landmarks or directions and closed my eyes in dismay. At least we got some food and a drink at the last stop. If this was a neighborhood progressive dinner, they forgot the food, and the hospitality sucked.

Some short time later we stopped along a curb at another house in the residential area. Out of the car, we were led up the short straight cement walkway in front and then into the house. Just inside the door we were stopped while the Iraqis yelled at each other and then we were pushed ahead into a smoky room.

Sitting around a table like the humorous poster picture of the five dogs playing poker were five men in the middle of some kind of a card game. Again, the exchange with our driver seemed to be "why did you bring them here?" "I don't know...we've been all over town...it's late, and we are beat..." Somehow in the dim light one of the guys noticed the dried blood on my face and neck and made a gesture like "get him out of here." And so, we went back outside.

Instead of getting in the car, we were led across the street and around to the back door of a white-frame house. In the moonlight, I caught a glimpse of a medical symbol on a sign. After some knocking a man came to the door and let us in. It was a doctor's exam room! The doc told me to sit up on the table and hold the light, and then he proceeded to work at cleaning the side of my neck and face while mumbling to himself in Arabic. Then, in pretty good English, he grimaced and said that I needed some stitches in my head. I politely asked that he "just clean it up, please. No stitches, thank you." I was certain this was a real doctor but I was too afraid of having him poke around in my neck with a needle at this time of night with me holding a flashlight. A bandage would be good enough.

Leaving the doctor's, we expected to be put back in the car. Instead, after crossing the street, they led us by small oil lantern through the yard around to the right to a long run-down building that seemed like a kennel, a stable, or at best, some kind of storage closets. On the backside, one of the guards opened a shaky wooden door and then the other pushed us inside. "Sit down," he commanded. "Toilet," I rebutted, hoping to get a look around. It was useless. He led me just two doors down to the left. This spot was as deserted as the rug place where we had stopped along the road.

Before locking us in, they put the lantern inside on a small tiled waist-shelf so they could watch us through the little open window in the door.

"This can't be the place," I pleaded to myself. "It can't end here."

I sat cross-legged against the hard stucco surface of the back wall facing the door; Grif was on my right against the other wall. The space was about three-by-four feet; it was filthy. Thrown on the dirt floor was an old coarse wool horse blanket slightly larger than a doormat. Outside we could hear the grunts of a guard who periodically looked in at us.

I was beyond exhaustion. This had to be a day in Hell: machine gunned on the Syrian border, a couple of hours sleep while chained to a cot, interrogated by the area commanders in Al Qaim, attacked by the mob in the village, the never-ending car trip to Baghdad; all the stops, all the same questions and now, stashed here in this kennel. Please God, let me be strong, I agonized. *For thine is the power and glory forever.*

The night chill turned to cold; I was freezing. In my weakened condition, I began to shudder and tried to rock back and forth as I embraced myself, pulling my knees against my chest. My whole body ached; unconsciously, I was moaning pitifully. Sometime later, I must have just passed out from exhaustion.

CHAPTER 10

Downtown

The sound of the door woke me. "Go! We go!" beckoned the soldier. It was morning (Wednesday, January 23). As I struggled to stand the bindings on my wrists were a painful reminder of our solemn situation; my body ached all over. Still, it was good to get up off that cold dirt floor.

We were led away to the right by two armed men. It seemed we were cutting through an area covered with tall pines behind the house. After maybe seventy-five yards or so we hit the end of a deserted street. I was glad that we apparently weren't condemned to this awful place and I remember how good the warm sun felt. In my thoughts the words, *the Lord will bless you and keep you. He will make his face shine upon you, and give you peace,* seemed all-telling.

In too short of time, a dirty white sedan drove toward us and stopped. Grif and I were blindfolded and pushed into the back seat with our knees on the floor. A blanket was thrown over us.

Soon, I could hear city sounds: buses, cars honking; we stopped frequently. As we rode along I felt we were finally headed for some kind of prison. Or maybe we would be held downtown in a hotel-like facility. My mind filled with images of the hostages in Beirut. Still, getting into a more formal system had to be better than this, if for no other reason than maybe they would feed us. Except for one hard-boiled egg, a few dates, some white crackers, and a little chicken, I hadn't eaten since Saturday evening (five days ago) before we briefed for the flight. That cup of chili con carne was only a memory now.

A sharp turn and we stopped. It was a gate. This time there was no belated explanation. The gate was opened and the driver pulled a short distance inside and came to a stop. The right rear door was opened and we were pulled out. "Quickly! Quickly!" commanded a richly accented voice. Through the bottom-side of my blindfold, I could see we were on what seemed like the top of a parking garage. The hatch-type steel door we entered required a step-over before we descended two flights of steps into a hallway. Down to the right I was pushed into sitting in a chair. Beyond us was another heavy door that kept opening and closing as people came in and out. I could tell Grif had been shuffling along behind me and was sitting nearby.

In a short time someone stopped, grabbed the left shoulder of my flightsuit, and pulled me along through the door. I sensed this was a large room where I was seated in front of a tribunal. I knew how beat up I felt inside; hopefully my dirty and bloody appearance reflected the same. The questions started more formally than the previous banter.

"What is your name? What is your nationality?"

Slowly and softly I responded, "Colonel David William Eberly. I am from United States." With such apparent injuries it might be only natural that I would be confused.

Then a zinger: "Why you come here and bomb us?"

I remembered our original story and stayed with it. Yes, I knew I could simply say my name, rank, and serial number but I didn't see myself as a prisoner. Slowly, I began again, "We didn't bomb you. We were flying in the West. . .electrical problems. . .bailout. . .walking. . .three days. . .trying to get help. . . ." They didn't seem impressed.

Quickly then, it turned political. "Your country. . . America attacked us. . . ,"

"Not United States, the United Nations. The coalition. . .because you invaded Kuwait. . . ." I said, almost boldly. Then I quickly remembered: don't be an ugly American. Be humble, but be right. In my mind, a vision of our flag. I had to be strong even if this was the end. And if so, it just didn't matter. Again the 23rd Psalm flashed through my mind. . .*I will fear no evil.* I had no idea who these men were but they were the enemy. I'm not going to be on the defensive; I can continue the fight, be on the offense, but without being offensive.

I can't remember how it ended, possibly with some sarcastic threat by the man in front of me about paying for all the killings by the Americans. Someone grabbed my collar; I was pulled out through a different door and told to wait. Then, through another door.

This was a smaller room, acoustically quieter even with two or three men talking. I could hear the faint sound of camera equipment running and could see from the bottom edge of my blindfold there were bright floodlights. Thank God, I said to myself. I felt if they took my picture our (intelligence) people would somehow get it and they (my family and the USAF) would know I was alive.

Roughly, I was pushed down on a stool against the wall

to my right and my blindfold was jerked off. Bedazzled, my eyes adjusted to the bright lights and I saw three men and some video camera equipment. The guy nearest me on my right was in uniform and had a nine-millimeter pistol. Another civilian stood in front of me, also to the right, while the third worked the camera. The civilian was holding a clipboard and appeared to be in-charge.

Then he started. "What is your name?"

"Colonel David William Eberly," I said.

"You are a war criminal. . .Ameriki!" he charged.

"No."

"What was your airplane?"

"F-15."

"You have been bombing our cities. . .women and children. You will tell us!"

"No," I said. With that, the guy on the right smacked my head.

Then he started over: same questions, same tactic. All the time the camera was running. Remorseful, I again realized I was not just giving my name, rank, and serial number but the principled exchange in the other room had somehow boosted my spirits. My inner emotions remained strong; I was going to keep my wits.

He got to the targets again, saying something about "…innocent women and children." So I responded, "No, chemical weapons storage facilities," figuring they'd never release that. And if they did, so much for the propaganda. This was not a popular decision. The spokesman's frustration was growing, and the guy to my right was eager to weigh in. Obviously I wasn't cooperating and they were not getting the story they intended. Now, there was some exchange between the spokesmen, and the guard pulled his pistol.

"We try again. . .you will cooperate!"

I stuck to my story.

Now the guy put the gun to my head. "You answer my questions or you die, here."

We had come to the end. In my mind I could picture a scene out of the movies where the side of my head would be blown out. I wondered if I would even hear the shot or feel anything. At least if they shoot me it will be on film. I didn't say a word—just kept my eyes open, stared at him, and prayed, *Thy will be done.*

Time stood still.

Then he barked again and the guy pulled back. This time we went through the questions again. Slowly, I responded with the same answers, nothing more. I was disgusted that I had failed to get to the target and that we had been shot down, but now God had given me the courage to continue the fight and to survive.

That was it. The guy callously retied my blindfold, slapped my head and pulled me out of the chair. Someone opened another door and I was led down several hallways and then told to "Sit, now!" Reliving the moment, my legs wobbled as I slid down against the wall.

I was somewhere along a corridor wall but I could smell food and hear the sound of metal plates and utensils. I sensed there were other people sitting on the floor nearby and began to cough and clear my throat. My noises were answered; Grif was there, too. Frequently, people would walk past us and purposefully kick my legs. I tried to ball up as inconspicuously as possible to blend into the baseboard crack.

Now out of the spotlight, it was time to try and check

the place out. The next time footsteps approached I called out, "Toilet. WC now, please!" Surprisingly, someone came to me and pulled me up by the collar. I stood and he led me down the hall, through a door, up some stairs. Then he pushed open another door before pulling off my blindfold. It was a European-style three-stalled bathroom with a urinal. Coyly, I stood at the urinal, and then turned around to the sink. There in the mirror I saw my facial injuries for the first time. My left jaw was swollen with a quarter-sized scab halfway to my ear. The gauze bandage around my neck was all stained on the left side with dried blood. Grif was right. It wasn't pretty but at least it didn't hurt. Even though my hands were cuffed, I tried to wash my face a little before the guard motioned me to come so he could put my blindfold back on.

Back in the hallway, the smell of food was evident. "Hungry, food, please," I said. And then miraculously, someone brought me a metal bowl of rice with some kind of meat and vegetables on top. This was terrific; I gobbled it down.

One haunting thought now echoed in my mind as I rolled over on my side: If we are downtown in some sort of military bunker, we are in a target! We have got to get out of here by dark. As warm as it is down here, dear God, this can't be the place.

I must have fallen asleep because I awoke when someone kicked me. "Quickly, quickly!" came the familiar demand. Now there were several of us being shuffled along. We went up some steps and then out through the same step-over door. The sudden cold air was chilling but refreshing. It was already dark. As they pushed me into another car, I thanked God we were getting away from that target. How unlucky it would be to be bombed by our own guys.

CHAPTER 11

The Old Jail

It was a short walk from the car—maybe twenty steps to a barred door beside a larger, iron double gate. Inside, the dim light from the guard's lantern cast eerie shadows on the stone walls along the deserted walkways. Around a corner to the left, then down two doors on the right, we stopped. My anxiety peaked. From behind, I felt the familiar push as I struggled to keep my balance. Someone jerked me around and grabbed my wrists; another unlocked the handcuffs and pulled off my blindfold before he pushed two wool blankets at me and then slammed the door behind me. The sound of the heavy key in the door lock signaled a solemn finality to my journey.

The feeling of having my hands free after being bound nearly two days was lost in the sense of terror I felt in the darkness and confinement of wherever I was. I closed my eyes and prayed for courage to face the unknown. Standing motionless, my ears strained for clues. I could still hear the guards and, opening my eyes, could see the glow of the lantern moving about. There were several other cell doors being slammed. Selfishly, I hoped Grif was here, too.

The warmth from the wool blankets felt good. I pulled

them around my shoulders like a shawl and then tentatively reached out to touch a wall. Cautiously, I moved toward the left and then scooted down the rough wall to sit. Touching the floor, I could feel it was either compacted dirt or maybe concrete. The other walls were just beyond arms reach.

Outside, around the corridor walkways the activity had stopped and the dim glow from the lantern disappeared with the muffled talking of guards. This was it—at least for now. I was emotionally beat, my body numb. Keeping one hand on the wall for orientation in the dark, I shook out one of the blankets to lie on the cold floor and then lay down with the other over me. Even lying longways in the cell, I couldn't stretch out. Besides it was too cold and the covers were too short. The guards' voices had now been replaced with the mournful crying of cats in the dark. At least they should take care of any rats. What a hole, I thought, but then caught myself. I am still alive. Thank you God.

Thursday, January 24, 1991

The sound of voices and the screech of the big gate woke me. They were welcome sounds because for the first time in days I had to urinate. I also felt an uncomfortable itch in my groin area. Two of the soldiers came my way in the corridor. "Toiletten, toiletten," I pleaded. The young guards stopped at my door and then one in a gray shirt unabashedly unlocked the cell and led me to a room at the left end of the corridor. What a nasty place, just a dirt floor area with a run-off to one side. There was a spigot but I was sure the water was tainted.

In the few steps along the walkway, I realized I was in the second of three cells in a row before a passage door farther down. All total there might be fifteen to twenty cells off the corridor around the outside of the rectangular courtyard.

From my view through the small foot-square barred window space in my door, I could see only a few feet in either direction in the corridor. Along the base of the opposite wall there were English and Arabic numbers; I could see a series of marks and knew I was "26." Across the narrow corridor I could see through a larger window space into the courtyard that was partially covered by a makeshift tin roof on my side. The double gate was at my left, ten to eleven o'clock. Above the roofline was the top of a dead tree. Small branches had fallen on the roof. The whole scene was right off the set in the deserted small western town from the movie, *The Last Picture Show.*

Inside the cell, conditions were appalling. We would have never left Ted, our Airedale, in such a place. The space was approximately four by five feet. There was another window in the back wall, but it had been secured outside with boards and chicken wire, plastic and cardboard on the inside. The walls were pealing stucco on brick with a potpourri of Arabic scratchings and rows of hash marks tallying the lifetimes of previous prisoners. Small busy critters on the dirt floor now detoured in criss-crossed fashion on their journeys trying to avoid my Gulliver-like presence. If this was it. . .well I guess I could have never imagined such a rat hole. Then to my thoughts came the words that Chaplain Hill used to start each sermon in the chapel at Seymour: "Good morning, Lord. And Lord, it is a good morning." I realized things could be much worse. I wasn't hanging upside down over an anthill, and so far, I was still on my way home.

The itch in my crotch, however, was getting more annoying, and I felt as though my hands were losing the feeling of touch. I unzipped my flight suit and turned toward the light. "Ugh!" My groin area was covered with a bright red rash and I could feel the itching extending behind my knees and along my sides. What ever was happening I only knew I had to fight the impulse to scratch or even touch the area. (I had early on decided I would keep my hands away from my face and mouth to avoid getting sick.)

This morning there seemed to be a lot more activity outside and noise in the distance than when we were brought in last night. In addition to the two young guards that had come by my cell there were a couple more at work in the walkway across the courtyard. Without trying to draw attention, I stood by my door straining to listen to every sound and see what was going on. Down the corridor to my right, it sounded like someone said something in English. I heard a door being opened and then the unsteady footsteps of someone approaching. Hesitating momentarily near my door, I waited to see if maybe it was Grif.

To my surprise, it was another American—an aviator! Quickly, I whispered as he shuffled by, "I'm Colonel Eberly, US Air Force." His eyes darted toward me as he moved on. God, did he look bad!

Coming back, he cautiously paused and briefly glanced toward my window. "I'm Lieutenant Zaun, Jeff Zaun, Navy, A-6s." I could see he was concerned about drawing the attention of whoever was watching him from down the hall.

Then, the sound of another door and someone else was coming my way. Again, another American in a flightsuit. I quickly identified myself and like before, when he came back, he looked my way and whispered, "Lieutenant Larry Slade, F-

14s." He too looked exhausted and like he'd been dragged through a dirt pile.

I couldn't imagine where Grif was but since these other guys were here, this must be the place and he must be here somewhere. Maybe Donnie Holland and Doc Koritz had miraculously survived the second night and were here, too. I remembered the stories from the Viet Nam guys and knew I had to start remembering names. "OK, Zaun, Slade, and hopefully, Grif." It was good that we had seen each other in case one of us didn't show up at the end. Briefly, I thought about Barbara and Timm and the others' families but quickly realized I couldn't dwell on them. I am here, they are there.

It was now maybe mid morning. The two guards were making rounds again, this time with a long-spouted pot. They unlocked my door and gave me some hot black tea. It warmed my hands and the first sweet sip seemed like a Thanksgiving feast. I was not about to question the unsanitary appearance of the cup.

"SHOOK-ran, SHOOK-ran," I said. The young soldiers seemed surprised and nodded. "I'm David," I said, pointing to my chest. "Your name?"

"Ali," responded the gray-shirted one. The other seemed caught off-guard and said something to scold the first as he locked my door and pushed him on. Maybe these guys could be corrupted, I thought. At least I had to start somewhere.

Staring at the stucco, I realized I needed to figure out what day it was and to make some kind of scratching of my own to keep track of the days. A calendar of some kind would help me and divert my attention from all those endless hash marks. As I searched in the dirt for something to mark with, I thought, hey, I won't be here that long. The war can only last a week or so before we level the place. If we have to be someplace, it's good we're at least out here in the boondocks, away from the city where we should be safe from the bombing.

Near the back window I found a prize rusty nail and then began to sort out the days. Flew Saturday night the 19th, Sunday morning got to the hill, Sunday night made contact with Cole, Monday heard the SAR, Monday night start for Syria, Tuesday early morning captured then start to Baghdad, overnight in the kennel, Wednesday taken downtown and then here. Today is Thursday, the 24th. Then as I marked off the days, the number "43" softly overcame my thoughts.

Suddenly there was activity by the gate; two guys were shuffling someone along. A big guy was led through our corridor and locked in a cell around the corner to my left. I couldn't tell for sure but it seemed he was on crutches. Got to get his name tonight.

The sun had taken away the shadows in the courtyard when the guards came back. It was Ali and his buddy. One by one they opened the doors. When they came to me I was handcuffed and then blindfolded and then led out of my cell and put in a front-to-back line with my hands on someone in front of me. His clothing felt like nomex and from his size I figured it was Grif. Maybe he was next door to my left. What's up, I wondered. Is this it? Are we all going home? Or was this old jail just another temporary stop—any place had to be cleaner than this.

Again, the car ride was accented with traffic sounds. We must be going back downtown, I thought. Maybe they were going to try again with the war criminal bit. Unless they are going to start pulling out my fingernails, they can't have much new to try. They already pulled the trigger yesterday.

Still, I realized I had only gotten this far because of God's help, and I prayed for continued physical and mental strength to face our captors...*for thine is the power and glory forever.* As we sped along, I also prayed for the Iraqis. Please give them the strength to be compassionate.

Our arrival was met with much less fanfare. Instead of being sequenced into some sort of tribunal, we were pushed into side-armed classroom chairs. The guys-in-charge were more intent on reviling and punching and would frequently smack one of us with a clipboard. From the sounds of the movements in the room it seemed that individuals were pulled out for interrogation one at a time. Without warning, I was jerked out of my chair. The voice of my interrogator was easily recognizable as the same guy from the photo shoot yesterday. Now, my apparent frustration with his questioning and the unattended appearance of my injuries reinforced the drama of my thespian performance.

"Don't you remember! I told you yesterday... we were alone. The planes are new. We were flying at night. . .our first sortie...the target was a chemical weapons storage facility. . .I don't know. I need a doctor."

On and on, around the same circle. It was logical that my head injuries and loss of blood would lead to fragile emotions and periodic incoherence. Still, my story was the same and since they had already pulled the trigger yesterday, we quickly came to an impasse. Smacking the back of my head wasn't going to make any difference. Finally, I was again relegated to the hallway and the kicks of passersby; fortunately my hands were cuffed in front.

The shuffling and moaning noises along the wall told me I was not alone. I could smell food and so it was time to beg. I hadn't had any water since yesterday. "MAI-ah, MAI-ah, we need drink please," I said as someone walked by. It worked! In broken and accented English someone said something about food and then another rattled some tin pans and seemed to be dishing up portions of the same rice mix we had the day before. Great, I thought to myself. If coming downtown means we get to eat and go to the bathroom, then OK. Just so we get out of here by dark before the bombing starts. After feeding, I asked to go to "WC." Sure enough, it was the same place.

Time dragged on until we were finally rousted from our wall cracks. Again, it was dark when we emerged outside before being stuffed in a car.

I sensed we had been taken back to the old jail. As the guard led me through the corridor I lightly put my right hand over on his forearm to steady my walk and to make human contact.

"Ali?" I asked.

"Yes," he said.

"Good. SHOOK-ran."

That night I counted six or seven cell doors being secured before the guards left. I knew Zaun, Slade, and yes, Grif was here. Plus, somebody down to the right who spoke Arabic. In the haunting quiet I stood at my door and called out in a whisper for Grif. He answered from just next door on my left. Selfishly, I was glad he was here. We talked for just a few minutes. To my right I could hear others whispering. In the darkness I spoke out: "This is Colonel Eberly. If you can hear me I want to pass on something General Horner told me when I met with him in December. 'Nothing up here is worth dying for.'" I think Slade said something in reply. With that I moved back and felt to my right to find my two blankets on the floor. It was already cold so I tried to ball up into a fetal position—laying on one folded blanket and covering with the other. The heat from the wool blanket ignited the torment of the incessant itching that was spreading to my legs and arms.

It felt like fire; I fought the urge to dig into the irritation on my stomach. My thighs and forelegs felt like they were being eaten by a thousand red ants. Frantically, I thrust out my legs and pulled up my pant legs exposing my bare skin to the cold. I must be allergic to this wool. Such a choice—I'm either going to freeze or go nuts scratching. Or maybe there were some bugs in that horse blanket the other night or maybe, there was penicillin in that crap the guy put on my neck. I wanted to scream and dig into my legs till they bled. *Please God help me.* I prayed as I gritted my teeth and clinched my fists.

Sometime in the darkness I fell asleep while listening to the cats banter on the roof.

Friday, January 25

I awoke to the same cold hard floor and four dreary walls. It was raining outside and the damp air chilled me to the bone. My hands felt puffy and my face seemed swollen. God, how will I get through today? Then, staring at the stucco, I remembered Chaplain Leon Hill. "Good morning Lord. And Lord, it is a good morning." My eyes focused on the peeling and chipping of the wall beside my beggar's pallet. The image looked like Ted's big rectangular head. To his left, I could make out the silhouettes of Barbara and Timm. Below him in the stucco the decay forged images that looked like a long line of circus animals—elephants with trunks, lions, bears on their back legs, chimps and even a giraffe. It was a happy sight, yet in some way we were all caged together. I strained to stand; the cold had penetrated my muscles. Still, I knew I must stretch and get up and move about to warm up. At eye level now, those incessant hash marks were a silent reminder of days to come.

As I scratched a "25" in the Friday space, I again thought of "43" and then remembered today was Barbara's birthday. What a bad day. She probably doesn't even know what's happened, but maybe that's good. Please Dear God, comfort her and Timm, I prayed. I visualized our kitchen and then realized they were still sleeping. It's OK; I can't worry about them. My thoughts were filled with the words to the old hymn, "Trust and obey for there's no other way. . . ." Other one-liners followed: "Faith of our Fathers" and "Amazing Grace." I knew I was not alone.

Now the guards came in through the gate. I did need to go to the bathroom—must have been the food and drink from downtown. Maybe we would get some hot black sweet tea again today before going back for interrogation.

The guards stopped along the way—the guy around the corner, then Grif, and finally to me. While going to the bathroom, I could see that I had a severe allergic reaction to something. The hives continued to spread. Reluctantly, I asked Ali, "Doctor, you bring doctor?" His reply: "Five minutes." I was concerned with exposing this vulnerability to the enemy but I had to get some relief.

Later, the guards came around again. This time when the door opened, Ali was holding some yellow clothing and the other guard had a bag of old tennis shoes. "Put on!" he said, as the second soldier looked at my feet and then handed me a pair of large sneakers. Reluctantly, I took off my boots and flightsuit. The psychological transformation was disheartening. The vestiges of my nobility were now stripped away. The yellow duck pants were far too large in the waist and the shoes, "Bo bo zekes" as Timm would call them, were missing laces and flapped like those of a circus clown. Strips of binding ripped from the blanket edging worked as shoestrings and a belt. I was glad I kept my T-shirt, long underwear bottoms and socks.

As I paced two-by-three steps, I again thought about Al Kharj. How I missed being there with the guys, working the flying schedule with Ray. We were a great team molded by the experiences of the last six months of living together at Thumrait (our initial deployment site in Oman). I thought about my last words to Hornburg as I passed him in the dark by the operations tent on the way to the jet.

But I was here, at least for a few days until the war was over. I needed to think about what I would say when we were released. The return of the Viet Nam War prisoners to Clark AB had been a big deal and more recently Barbara and I had watched intently as Terry Anderson and the other hostages from Lebanon had come through Wiesbaden, Germany. While I certainly did not imagine we would see any such fanfare, I did hope there would be a chance to publicly say "thank you" before we headed back to Saudi. Almost smiling, I could picture the scene. Getting off the airplane, making a few brief comments and then starting to walk on when someone would say: "Now that you've been released, what are you going to do?" I would stop, look at the camera and say: "We are going to take our families to Disney World!"

My optimism, however, was frequently cursed with the

lyrics of the Buddy Holly tapes I had been playing during the past several months. The contradiction to my belief in a quick release was the echoing of his voice singing "…that'll be the day when I die…"

Sometime after noon they brought us some rice and bread. It wasn't like downtown but it was something. Plus, they gave me a plastic pitcher with some water. The compromise was between getting something to drink and then having to go to the bathroom.

Loud music from outside our world rolled over the compound wall interspersed with light traffic sounds. We were near a street but not downtown. I had investigated the security of the boarded window in the cell—it was leading nowhere, at least for now. As for rolling out of a vehicle on what seemed to be a daily pattern of going downtown for interrogation, that too, offered little chance for a successful escape. Although I missed the real bathroom, that was fine with me considering I was convinced it was only a matter of time before that place was bombed. Now, for the first time we heard the sound of the call to prayer echo across the sky.

Darkness brought one last trip to the toilet and some water. It was becoming apparent that the plastic water container was going to have to substitute for a urinal. Either I kept some water and urinated in a corner or tried to keep my dirty floor dry for sleeping. As for seeing a doctor in "five minutes," maybe tomorrow.

When the guards left, I went to the door to whisper to Grif. We compared the names of guys we had seen and then talked about being cold. I told him about my hives and that I wished all I had to worry about was keeping warm. As before, there wasn't much to say before we said good night. I briefly thought of Barbara and imagined the warmth of the sun outside our home. I prayed that someone had remembered her birthday—and then tried to distance myself from the vision.

Lying on the floor, my skin began to crawl. Even my back was sensitive to moving on the rough floor and I wanted to back up to the wall and rub against it like a bear on a tree. Tonight it seemed as though the torment had spread to my feet—the worst case of athletes' foot. I threw off the blanket and frantically took off my shoes and socks, exposing my feet to the cold. I dared not start scratching for fear of starting them to bleed and then risking infection from my dirty hands. My legs too were afire. I couldn't stand it any longer. With my long underwear to cover my skin I began to dig my fingers into my legs. God, I'm going nuts! Please, please let this pass. I pleaded in prayer. Finally the pain from digging into my legs surmounted the itch and I fell asleep listening to the screeching of the fighting cats.

Saturday, January 26

I didn't make it through the night. The extra water had forced me to give up the sanity of my plastic pitcher for a urinal. I figured I could rinse it out if there was still water from the spigot in the toilet area.

My hands were itching now too and I knew it was only time before this stuff came up my neck to my face. When the guards did come in, I asked again for a doctor—same reply, "five minutes."

Late morning a guard came to my cell with the now recognizable kit of handcuffs and blindfold. Once shackled, I was led out—this time there was no queue. Instead I was led out the gate to the right and down a narrow, wobbly walkway some fifty steps to another building before being guided to an armed wooden desk chair. Not surprising, the voice of the interrogator was the same.

He confirmed my name and then wanted to talk about the bombing again. Once again, I told him it was "nice to hear your voice again" and then I asked for some water and told him we weren't getting anything to eat. He said that the bombing had destroyed the markets and that food had been strictly rationed. He did give me some water though. Each time I drank the whole glass and then, with my swollen hands in obvious view, I made a plea that "we have injured guys who need to see a doctor." He acted surprised that I knew there were others. Inside I felt good. I wasn't going to be intimidated. If I was the senior guy, it was my responsibility no matter the consequence. Doggedly I pressed the issue but realized we were getting nowhere—he wanted answers first and was not interested in any Geneva Convention protocols. I was visibly injured and focused on getting us more food and water and some medical help. Fortunately, he did not let his emotions overcome his apparent frustration with me beyond the familiar threat that I had "better start cooperating." When he finally yelled for someone outside, I was emotionally relieved.

For the first time since being in prison, I was glad to get back to my cell. I don't know what time it was, but two soldiers were bringing some food around. I could hear each door screech as they stopped along the way and scooped dinner from the bucket. When they got to me it seemed like a feast—another answered prayer. They gave us a cup of lentil soup and a small piece of pita-type bread. Never mind the problem that I had to use my water cup—food was food.

Over by the gate it sounded like there were three or

four men talking. They entered the corridor to my left and then paused at each cell. Maybe it was the Red Cross, I thought. When they opened my door one of the men was dressed in civilian clothes. He said, "I am a doctor, are you well?" Holy smokes! I couldn't believe it; I wanted to cry.

"Please, I need your help." As I said something about "the wool," I extended my hands, dropped my pants so he could see my groin and then, almost whispering, told him I needed some anti-histamine pills and some benadryl cream. He nodded and half-smiled and then said he would come back later. I wanted to ask him about the war but instead simply asked about his family. He explained that he was British—that he was working in a hospital downtown. All I could do was hope and say, "Thank you for caring."

Surprisingly, he did come back. As the guard opened the door, I looked eagerly at his hands for a bottle of pills. Instead, I saw a syringe.

"Doc, what about my pills?"

I can't remember his reply but I wasn't about to argue. As I started to roll up my sleeve, he said it must go in my rear. I dropped my pants and turned to lean against the doorframe. Standing there I thought to myself, how ironic, I'm going to live through this and then someday get home and die of AIDS. Before he left, he gave me an envelope of five pills and a small tube of cream.

That night I told Grif about the shot and my fear of infected needles. But then, it just didn't matter. I would have gone insane scratching without help. What a day it had been.

Sunday, the 27th

My system for recycling the water pitcher was by necessity working. And, if there was a trend developing after three days, at least things weren't getting worse. I was intent on following any activity at the gate or in the center courtyard. Most of my waking thoughts were spent praying; all my time was spent pacing to keep warm.

We were being fed a little once a day. There was a little water and these young guards were showing some compassion. Possibly, if this drags on, I thought, we can get some information as to where we are and maybe work on these back windows.

About mid-day, the doctor showed up again with another shot. I told him the cream had helped last night but that I had still broken down and dug into my legs. He told me it would just take time and that I had to keep from getting the sores infected. Humorously, I thought how the torment was meant to keep my mind off the puritanical existence.

That night, as the air raid sirens wailed in the distance, I prayed for courage and the emotional strength to survive.

Monday, the 28th

It was a bright and sunny day outside. The sun slowly rebuffed the chill of the morning. Ali had made the rounds earlier with a paper bag of small bars of soap. This was great. I don't think anyone thought that hot showers would follow but at least we could wash our hands under the trickle of water.

Beyond the always-appreciated trips to the toilet area and some food around mid-day, it was to be just another day in the old jail. I worked on my speech as I paced and maintained vigilance on any activity. I hadn't seen anyone else come in. Maybe we had been the only ones shot down; surely the ground forces must be plowing through toward Baghdad.

After feeding time, Ali came back and motioned me to follow—no blindfold no cuffs. We went to the end of the corridor and then he opened a door that led into the center court. "It's OK," he said as he motioned for me to go out.

Cautiously, I stepped into the sun. Was this a trap? I took it all in. If someone was going to jump me, it wasn't obvious. I could only imagine that as the senior guy, I was about to be the entertainment—to be beaten or killed as an example. Instead, nothing. I moved to the center thinking that while the allies didn't know we had lost our flightsuits at least there might be some overhead photography that would capture my image. After what seemed like fifteen minutes, Ali motioned for me to come back. My cell now looked smaller and dirtier than before. Still, the sun had given me new strength and energized my thoughts. I had a lot to be thankful for—I was still alive.

Tuesday, the 29th

The trickle of water had stopped—how fate played with our emotions. Now soap, no water. We were better off before. Anxiety was somehow the evil twin of boredom. I tried to stay alert and focused. Only prayer eased my torment.

Wednesday, the 30th

I woke with the same anxiety and fought to keep my grip on the positive. Eagerly, I sought my chance to go to the toilet area—still no water. *Please God, help us,* I prayed. We could be in real trouble.

Marking off the day, I realized I was in the box under the "23." We had been here for a week.

Late morning another American was brought into the courtyard and forced to stand under the tin roof opposite my cell. Someone asked his name.

"Captain Michael Craig Berryman," he crisply responded.

From my cell door window I could barely see him. His voice was strong but he too looked battered. With professional resolve his answers held to the strict limits of the Code of Conduct and drew sharp physical responses from his interrogator. He was a Marine. Disappointingly, I realized that in my own interactions with these guys I had not simply responded with "name, rank, and serial number." They had taken away my amour and put me in a box but in my mind I hadn't accepted the role of being a prisoner of war. Instead, whether it was stubbornness or stupidity, I had still been trying to continue the fight—taking air power jabs whenever I could. They were the bad guys. Unprovoked, they had attacked Kuwait and, without cause, they had shot Scuds into Tel Aviv.

As I stood in the dark that night staring blankly out my cell door into the courtyard, I thought about the new guy, Berryman. His responses echoed in my ears. I was proud of him; I envied his courage. We were a long way from home; we were tired, hungry, and beat up but I had felt God was indeed keeping watch over us. The "power of positive thinking" that guided my mother's life now served as my beacon in this new trial of Desert Storm.

Thursday, January 31st

Finally, I had gotten through the night without insanely reacting to my hives. The shots and cream had helped—it was not spreading.

I hoped the interrogators would eventually give up on us and that we would simply be left alone in this grunge pit. It all seemed relative. We were getting some food once a day and although there was no water in the toilet area, Ali and the young soldiers would give us a drink at feeding time. The torment from my hives was lessening although I still had the odd fit of rage some nights. I spent my whole day pacing to keep warm and to reduce the anxiety of the endless moments. Between praying and working on a release speech, I kept my mind occupied with the scattered lyrics of Buddy Holly and the one-line verses of old hymns I had grown up with at Epworth Methodist Church.

That night as Grif and I whispered and traded our usual "how you doing?" I made some reference to getting through the next few days. I told him that we were just a few days away from February 2nd, the day Buddy Holly was killed and "the day the music died." His response was more reflective of what's important in life. It was his anniversary this weekend. In reference to the harassment during the interrogations, he said, "A good day is when you just see these four walls." I tried to be positive and talk about the future. Grif was on the list to go to staff college at the end of the summer, so to imply that we'd be free soon, I told him I was sure he'd enjoy the more relaxed schedule of school and the extra time to be with his family. With that we said good night and I felt for my pallet.

It seemed like the middle of the night when I awoke to a scurrying of activity. I can't remember hearing the gate or the other doors but suddenly my cell door was opened and a bright lantern was blinding my eyes. My blanket was yanked away and I found myself nearly airborne as my hands and feet were cuffed and a tight rag tied around my head. Unsteadily,

I was led around the corridor and out the gate. Instead of a surprise interrogation down the walkway as I suspected, I was put into what seemed like a small English bus—two steps up— and pushed into a half seat. I sensed there were others on the bus but I was sitting alone. The only sounds were the smacking of heads and the sharp demands of the Arabic voices. Just as many times before, the words of the 23rd Psalm filled my thoughts: *Yea though I walk through the valley of the shadow of death, I will fear no evil. God help us, I prayed. Give us the strength and courage to get through this. For thine is the Kingdom and power and glory. Amen.*

Above left: Col. Ray Davies and Col. Eberly. Above right: Col. Eberly and LtCol. Steve Turner, 336th Squadron Commander. Below: General Schwarzkopf (far left) visits before the war. Also pictured are (from left to right) Col. Hal Hornburg, (fourth from left) Col. Pat Schauffele, David Eberly and Col. Ray Davies. (Photo courtesy of U.S. Army)

Flier's dream is shot down

By Michael Hedges
THE WASHINGTON TIMES

Eberly

EASTERN SAUDI ARABIA — On a windy day early this month, Col. David William Eberly stood in the shadow of his F-15E Eagle fighter-bomber and discussed how he felt about the prospect of flying it into combat.

"When I left the house on Aug. 9, my wife said, 'Well, you've been waiting 20 years to do this.' She was right," the 43-year-old flier said.

Col. Eberly spoke to the media again last week.

But this time it was an Iraqi television camera he was facing, and the much more subdued officer was describing how he was shot down and captured by Iraqi forces.

"I believe I was wounded in the neck either in . . . the plane, or when I hit the ground with the parachute."

Col. Eberly said in the Iraqi TV interview, which was monitored by the British Broadcasting Corp.

On Monday, the Pentagon included Col. Eberly, of Brazil, Ind., as one of seven U.S. pilots officially listed as prisoners of war in Iraq. Concern for his safety has grown as Iraqi radio reports that one allied pilot has died and others have been wounded in bombing raids over Iraq.

When we spoke, Col. Eberly was less than two weeks from realizing his ambition of flying in combat and less than three weeks from being shot down.

The colonel — the deputy operations officer of the 4th Tactical Fighter Wing — seemed a pilot from central casting. He was of medium height and trim, with eyes that penetrated even from behind his aviator sunglasses.

He replied articulately to a range of questions but clearly was most at ease when he spoke about his plane and the art of flying it.

Looking ahead to the U.N. set Jan. 15 deadline for Iraq to withdraw from Kuwait, the colonel evoked the calm of a seasoned professional and what now sounds like a note of eerie prescience.

"We've gone through a lot of peaks already," he said. "As new guys come in, I tell them, 'You are going to go through an emotional roller coaster.' We don't anticipate dates. We anticipate the next sortie we fly."

He said then he believed "the first combat will be easier than the training the guys have gone through."

As with most of the pilots here, Col. Eberly placed near fanatical faith in his training. He spoke of the Red Flag exercise in which pilots attempted to duplicate the first 10 missions of the war.

Pointing to his F-15, he said, "That is a $40 million aircraft. It demands that when someone finishes his training, he can do the job of flying the airplane."

Col. Eberly held little hope at that time that the war could be avoided.

"I see this as a chance to serve," he said. "If we never drop a bomb and he [Iraqi President Saddam Hussein] withdraws, we have deterred aggression."

But the war came, and Col. Eberly flew a bombing run on the first day of combat. "I think it's been a good start," he said afterward.

He said that he saw some Iraqi MiG interceptors and that intense anti-aircraft fire "just lit up the sky."

Along with other pilots, Col. Eberly was highly optimistic after that first raid. But he warned that Iraq "still has formidable defenses, and we're after every piece of that. Each one of the targets is well defended."

A few days later, he went up on another mission and did not return.

Before the war, Col. Eberly said that after spending more than five months in Saudi Arabia, it felt like "the 22nd mile of the New York Marathon. We are rounding the corner."

A fellow pilot, Maj. Steve Turner, said that "it will be two different wars. One guy will see nobody, and one guy will see everybody. For that poor guy, it'll be a pretty wild ride."

After 20 years of waiting, the wild ride ended for Col. Eberly.

Opposite page, top: A newspaper account of Eberly's downing. Opposite page, bottom: Escape and evasion map: Al Qaim area in Northwestern Iraq. Above: General Powell and Secretary Cheney welcome Eberly and Griffith upon return to Andrews AFB. (Courtesy of Department of Defense) Below: The Eberlys arrive home at Seymour Johnson AFB. (Courtesy of U.S. Air Force)

Above: Brazil, Indiana, honors Eberly's return with a parade. Below: Timm, Barbara and David with his mother, Evelyn and step-father, Bill Wallace.

Above: David and Barbara with son, Timm in April 1991, six weeks after his return. Below: The POWs reunite for their 6-month medical checkup.

CHAPTER 12

The Builtmore

The urgency of our apparent kidnapping and the rough demeanor of our handlers heightened the tension of the situation. This was not Ali or his young cohorts nor was it a Delta Team rescue.

Why were we being taken downtown at this time of night? Maybe our ground forces were closing in; maybe we were shields being rousted into place. Surely we wouldn't be released in the middle of the night. What had changed? I wondered.

The little bus slowed then turned to the right before stopping. With the doors open, the cold night air made me shiver. I sensed the others were being taken off first. Doors were slamming and it sounded like we were being transferred into cars. Someone grabbed my arm and pulled me off my seat toward the door. I braced myself, grasping for his arm; I was afraid I would twist my still swollen ankles falling down the steps. One step later, I was pushed face-first into the back seat of a small car before it jolted forward. We couldn't have gone a hundred feet around a circle to the left when we stopped and I was pulled back out by the collar. Two guys grabbed me by the upper arms and hurried me forward. "Quickly. Move," directed the stern voice.

I sensed we were under a portico. Passing through double doors, I suddenly had the uneasy feeling that this was a hospital. With my hands cuffed in front, I bent over for protection from any punch to the stomach. My mind raced to the thoughts of the Nazi medical experiments and the inhumane Iraqi treatment of the Iranians. From the slit under my blindfold I could see we were going down a tiled hallway covered with a rubber mat. Then, into a small elevator to the second floor. Now a longer walk in a similar hallway where I felt the presence of others off to the sides. This could be bad, I thought.

For a second it sounded like the guy on my right was opening the heavy latch of a freezer door. I was pushed forward but stumbled on a large metal strip along the bottom of the doorway. Now one step inside, I hesitated as the door was quickly slammed and locked behind me. I felt an eerie danger sensation: my mind's eye saw that I was standing on the edge of the concrete ledge on the exposed side of bombed-out high-rise building. Even the air felt different and the noises seemed like I was outside. Was the idea that I tumble to my death when I supposedly tried to escape in the dark?

Finally, I slowly leaned to my left—there was a wall. Using it for balance, I inched forward so I could squat down. This is it, I said to myself. This is where we are staying.

Now my senses shifted, I could hear activity in the hallway—cell doors opening and closing—but the acoustics told me this place was solid. I strained to hear any outside noises and then decided I was not going to fall off the edge of the building. As I lifted the bottom of my blindfold more, I prayed there would be at least some sliver of light to give dimension to this void and keep the walls from suffocating me. Thank God, there was. In front of me a very dim horizontal bar of moonlight crept into my crypt.

Suddenly my door was being unlocked. When it opened briefly someone took off my handcuffs and leg chains and then tossed in a blanket. My plea for "WC?" was met with a sharp "No!" That was it. Slam.

Friday, February 1st

Daylight brought the stark reaffirmation to last night's sensations—this was no makeshift hotel room but neither was it a hospital. This was a real prison, no apparent tin pan hut off an alley like the old jail. The bad news, I decided, was that we might have missed our best opportunity for escape.

In the hallway it sounded like someone was mopping the floor. I pressed my ear against the door hoping to hear some English. Instead there were voices—maybe two or three men talking and a radio with loud Arab music. From their tone I decided it was best to wait them out.

This cell was all red brick with a concrete floor and measured approximately five by eight feet. The steel door had a smaller horizontal viewing door at eye level. There was a four-foot high divider on the window end. This short wall had a three-foot space in the middle and separated an area designed for a toilet and shower spigot. In reality the ceramic toilet was smashed and covered with a small piece of plastic dropcloth; the luxury shower was a bent pipe. Neither had running water. The only trickle came from a spigot beside the toilet. Considering all this there was good news in that even though it was already clogged and would not flush it was better than my dual-purpose pitcher. Plus, I had a rather clean green and white striped blanket and I wasn't sharing the floor with a variety of bugs.

The other good news was the availability of daylight. High on the outside wall was a deep-set window measuring roughly ten inches by five feet. Bolted against the cut out was a metal grate with one-inch flat louvers covering a heavy gage chicken wire. I couldn't tell for sure whether there was even glass in the space but I assumed the cold air settling on me was coming from the outside. In addition there was a recessed dim light with a plastic fixture covered with a metal grate in the wall next to the door. Unfortunately, the guards controlled the switch and only turned it on infrequently.

Markings on these walls told a similar story—humans had been caged here for many many days. I was not here to set a new record. Still I needed to recreate my calendar. God, I hated to start a new month. As I looked for a space to etch my seven-day boxes, I tried to convince myself there was no need to make room for March.

Suddenly I realized that in the bug out last night my nail for scratching on the wall and my remaining pills and cream were left in the corner of my cell. What a stupid mistake. At least I had kept all my clothes and was sleeping with my shoes on. From now on I stay packed. Everything I accumulate stays in my pockets. And I take my blanket.

One problem with this place being cleaner was the lack of useful scraps. Someone before must have had some soap because on the top of the small divider wall was an accumulation of what I would describe as dish residue. What a treasure! By scraping my fingernail back and forth over the area I put together a small ball the size of a marble. Then by gently rubbing it directly under my nose I could savor its sweet smell.

There were no nails or even rocks like before but eventually, I worked a small screw free from the drain plate and marked today's date on the wall. As usual the number "43" floated into mind and then as my spirits sank, I remembered another song from my childhood days at church camp: "It's me, it's me, it's me oh Lord, standing in the need of prayer. . . ." If ever I needed to feel His presence, it was now. *Give me the strength to get through this day,* I prayed.

Unknowingly, I had begun pacing just as in the old jail. Around and around, two steps by three steps, I was lost in prayer and song. The shadow on the wall of my blanket-draped figure looked like E.T.

Finally about mid afternoon some guy—not military—opened my little viewing door. He wanted to know my name. I told him and then asked for water, "MIA-ah." He said, "Five minutes. Sit down."

Sometime later I heard the sound of a wobbly-wheeled metal cart coming down the hall. Each time it would stop I heard the opening and closing of a little cell door. When it got to me my little door opened and a guy looked in and then said, "Bowl." I looked at his puzzled face peering in and said: "I don't have one—no bowl." He slammed the door. A couple minutes later he came back, opened the door, and handed me a plastic K-mart-type dog bowl with about a cup of tomato-based soup broth. "SHOOK-ran," I said, as he slammed the little door again and moved on.

That night I missed my whisper with Grif. His phase about "just seeing these four walls" had new meaning. I didn't know where he was but I hoped we had all moved. In case of a rescue, we'd all be here together.

By dark, I was exhausted. It had been a traumatic day

with all the new sounds in the hall and the additional distance I had walked. As I curled up on the cold floor, I thought of Barbara and Timm and Ted. I envied his thick soft LL Bean dog bed. The tingling itch of my hives reminded me of the cream I'd left behind. Lying on my right side against the door side wall I brought my legs up tight, pulled the blanket over my head, and used my fist as a pillow. I began with the Lord's Prayer and thanked God for the food we had gotten today. Saying those rote phrases as I had since childhood I suddenly realized I had cause to change some—to make them more personal. I said aloud, "Our Father, I know you are with me here. Thank you for the food you gave us today. Forgive us for our sins and bless the men who watch us. For thine is the kingdom, the power and the glory forever. And please comfort Barbara. Give her the peace to know I'm OK."

I was already asleep when the air raid sirens went off. It was as though they were right outside the building. Then the AAA. They had to be firing from our building. Although I couldn't see it directly, the action resonated through my window area like fireworks on the Fourth of July. In the distance it sounded like explosions. I huddled against the wall. All I could think of was the phase: *thy will be done.*

Saturday, February 2nd

It had been two weeks now—fourteen days since we had been shot down. The deserted quiet in the hallway ended with the arrival of new guards. Somehow I could smell their hot tea and could hear sounds of what must be sweets and dates in a paper bag. God, I was hungry.

Their radio broke the calm. The news in Arab babble was tormenting—if only we knew how it was going. The music was worse but did help mask the irritating sound of a heavy-duty motor running outside.

Around mid-day a civilian opened my door. While another watched, he chinched on the handcuffs and then a blindfold. This time we went left down the corridor and then down some stairs to right for one floor. Inside a room I was pushed into a straight-backed desk chair.

I sat with my hands in clear view to expose the swelling and irritation. Even though they felt like I was wearing boxing gloves, I tucked my fingers to avoid having them smashed. Sitting made the back of my legs itch and lowered my head making it more accessible to cuffing. Also, since I couldn't bend forward, my shins were more exposed.

"David William, I am going to ask you some questions. You will answer."

It's the same voice! I cocked my head slightly and struggled to whisper, "Oh, hello again." Then I asked for water. "Please, MAI-ah." Someone poured a glass and bumped the glass against my hands. Frantically, I drank the whole glass and reached out blindly to set it on the desk in front of me. Then he started with the same old line of questioning about targets and capability.

From my perspective behind the mask, I had visibly deteriorated. My hands were swollen and red, I was disheveled, and had two weeks of beard growth. It seemed to me, we had been locked away to starve to death. The guards wouldn't come when someone pounded on his door for water or attention. All we heard was, "No, sit down" or "Five minutes."

Hearing the familiar voice I decided today was my day to take the offensive. After all, what were they going to do: threaten to kill me or throw me in a dark cold cell and not feed me?

"We need help," I started. Slowly and cautiously, I continued, "We aren't getting enough food, no water. . .we need blankets...it's very cold...we were better in the other prison. These guards aren't taking care of us. I know we have some who need a doctor. Please, help." My pleas were again met with threats and the normal whacks to the head. I guess I was too pitiful to pursue because I was soon jerked back to my cell.

Later that afternoon I heard the feeding cart coming down the hall. I was grateful for anything but knew it was probably as good as it was going to get. One feeding a day is better than no feeding. The only problem was not having two bowls or a cup for a drink—it was either one or the other. Hearing the arrival of the cart reminded me of my college days in the Delt House at Indiana. At night, when we pledges would be seconded to our rooms for study table, some delivery guy would come to the house around nine selling prepackaged sandwiches and snacks. He would open the door to the first floor and announce his arrival. Smiling inside, I wanted to yell out: "Sandiman, food on one!"

When my little door did open, I was standing there, my blanket draped over my head, ready with my bowl. My eagerness was often dashed by the antics of a dastardly guy in a black business suit. Reluctantly he dished out a ladle of broth. My request for more—"Again?" was answered by a smirk as he took a little of the portion back. Then as he positioned my bowl to slide through the opening, he said, "President Bush" and spit at me. "SHOOK-ran," I said. Then he tore the piece of pita-type bread in two and gave me only half before he slammed the door. No drink today either! Comparing him to a maitre d', I wanted to yell after him, "and that's why I don't tip you (you s.o.b.)!"

I sat my bowl on the floor so it wouldn't spill and then slid down against the side wall. This day, by comparison, the broth was almost too hot to drink. My hands savored its warmth as I held the warm bowl and bread like communion elements while I thanked God for his blessings.

As the dim outside light turned from gold to gray I recalled how tough the day had been. Mastering wits during another interrogation, very little to eat, no water, and the lingering symptoms of my allergic reaction. I was exhausted and decided to give in and lay down early.

Sometime after dark in the wavering of the air raid siren, I became conscious of the sound of an in-bound, low-flying airplane. The following explosion was almost instantaneous—it hit so very close. Our building seemed to sway like a young sapling in the wind. Outside, in the corridor, the guards were yelling and cursing. I held my breath as I pulled my legs to my chest and waited for another explosion. Nothing. It must have been a cruise missile. Hey guys, it's us, I said to myself. Now, our maximum prison doesn't seem so safe. Why don't our guys know where we are? I thought.

As the last rounds of the warning siren echoed across the city, I rolled over—this time nestled more deeply in the wall crack as though it could provide some protection from another strike. Outside, the incessant sound of that irritating motor droned on.

Later, I woke again to the distinctive sounds of a rolling bucket, mopping and wringing, and casual chatter. It was a cleaning crew. Why couldn't they do this during the day? I thought. Why do they have to make noise at night? No wonder this place doesn't have a AAA rating.

As they moved closer down the corridor, I could hear the opening and closing of the little feeding doors. Curious, I sat up, my eyes fixed in the dark. Then someone turned on my light and opened my little door. I stood and saw an Arab wearing a traditional red and white checked ghutra with black agall like I had seen on my trip to town at Al Kharj in Saudi. He smiled and handed me two pieces of warm bread and then in good English asked if I needed some water. "Yes, yes," I quickly replied as he held up a bottle. "But I have no cup." He walked away and then came back with a glass filled with water. "SHOOK-ran," I said. Then he asked: "Do you need anything?"

"No, thank you," I said. And then, as he closed, the door I added, "God bless you."

I couldn't believe it. My thoughts were tumbling; my emotions spilling over. The Saudis have found us! They are masquerading as a cleaning crew and will come every night to secretly give us food and water and to check on us. We are going to make it.

In all this fantasy I recalled the scene in the movie we had watched while still in Oman where Lawrence of Arabia has finally amassed his Bedouin army and they triumphantly declare they are heading to Aqaba. Like Lawrence, I too, was now emotionally charged—it was the best I had felt yet. Ravenously, I ate half the bread—saving the other—and then curled up in my blanket as I gratefully thanked God for sending these kind people with food and water. For the first time I went to bed with something in my stomach and with renewed hope.

Sunday, February 3rd

In prison, waking was the transition from the comfort of unconsciousness to cold and guarded anticipation. It began with the sensation of the hard concrete floor and the decision to open my eyes and lift the edge of my blanket. If there was no noise and if there was no light, the black void would send an unnerving signal triggering a claustrophobic-type imbalance. My first prayer was simple: *Good morning Lord, and Lord it is a good morning. Give us the strength and courage to make it through this day—keep me sane.* Finally, lifting the edge of my blanket my eyes grasped the dull beam of gray light. If it was a sunny day the beam would focus into a sharp horizontal line at the 21st row of bricks on door wall and then move too quickly down toward the floor before disappearing. Morning was the lightest time of the day.

From my calendar I saw it was Sunday. With my senses tuned to the activity outside my cell I allowed my mind to wander briefly home to my childhood. Sunday was always special. Church at Epworth followed by Sunday dinner at my grandparents with fried chicken or noodles, mashed potatoes and gravy, with fresh apple pie. I could still see my grandfather turning the crank to make homemade ice cream. Frequently, my cousins would come over from Plainfield or we would meet them at a lake and go boating. What great memories to relive.

On the ledge I saw my glass with some water and remembered the kindness of last night's visitor. Looking at the glass I remembered the old saying about how different people look at a glass—half empty or half full. To the other prisoners and me, it's now just a drink of water. And, inside my shirt another treasure: the remains of the bread. Sparingly, I tore off a small piece and followed it with a drink. I can always hide the bread but if it sounds like there is a chance to get some water, I want to have an empty glass. Likewise, if I hear a guard approaching I will always stop pacing, sit down against the wall with my head covered, and present a humble, non-threatening appearance.

Today, bolstered by the optimism from last night, I decided to explore the possible weaknesses of the window area. I figured if I could get the grate off maybe there would be enough space to wiggle out. My only makeshift tool, however, was the drain plate (the plumbing parts were missing from the broken toilet and the water pipe extension was solid). It seemed quiet in the corridor so I climbed up on the dividing wall and leaned over to try to examine the louver fasteners. The first thing I discovered was that there was glass behind the grate and wire. So why the cold air? Second, my four-inch round drain plate was no tool for unscrewing or even prying. The window inset space was at least two feet thick so I couldn't see the ground or any trees. From the activity outside though it did seem like I was near a parking area or driveway. I had connected the sound of an arriving vehicle with the arrival of our food; our feeder was an outsider. Maybe the whole thing had been contracted out. Humorously I wondered, where's Marriott when we need them? Why not MREs? Oh, for even a cold lunch pack.

Considering my apparent closeness to the guards' position, I figured I was just above and to the side of the main entrance. Now I could distinguish the recognizable sounds of men starting a generator. And then I understood. Cold air was blowing out of a vent above the recessed wall light. They were using generator power to cool the building and thereby lower the heat signature.

Suddenly a voice yelled at me. I had gotten too engrossed in the outside and let my senses shift. Now a guard was looking at me through the little door. "Sun," I said, as I huddled on the divider. "Warm," pointing to the now bright rays.

"Sit down!" he ordered. So I quickly slid down and then shivering said: "Cold, need blanket."

"Five minutes," he curtly replied as he slammed the door. I was lucky this time.

I resumed my pacing and tried to be more alert to any approaching footsteps. Slowly my concerns were again overcome by the lyrics of hymns from my youth. "Amazing Grace," "Blessed Assurance," "Faith of Our Fathers," and others. Although still sensitive to any noise in the hallway the one-to-two line verses were a diversion from the isolation and frustration of confinement. I would walk clockwise two hundred times and then reverse direction. After two sets, I rested briefly and then did some push-ups and sit-ups. At one point I figured I was doing around five miles a day. I wanted to be ready if the chance came for an escape or if some force rescued us. Plus the walking was strengthening my sprained ankles.

Later, after feeding time, I heard water gurgling in the pipes and found there was a small stream available from the spigot beside the toilet. I was really thirsty but figured it was probably tainted so I put my food bowl under the stream and slowly collected enough to pour in the toilet; it gravity flushed. Then I rubbed my soap ball over my wet hands and for the first time gently felt the back of my neck. There was a huge quarter-sized scab imbedded in my hair. Just give it time, I thought. It doesn't hurt, and the interrogators haven't exploited it.

Even though I didn't have a watch, the attack pattern at night was predictable. Just after dark the air raid sirens would wail their warbling alert and then the anti-aircraft artillery tracers would light up the sky. In the distance, I could hear explosions. Since the first night downtown near the action, I had begun to picture the historical depiction of Francis Scott Key at dawn and quietly repeated the lyrics to our "Star Spangled Banner": ". . .bombs bursting in air." As a precaution after the near-by cruise missile hit, I always sat against the wall with my blanket over my head. Then after the steady all-clear siren I would feel my way over to the toilet and urinate before curling up with my blanket. I thought it was amusing—like the end of the super bowl—when everyone goes to the bathroom, except here the water company didn't worry about any flushing.

February 4ᵗʰ Just another day

My journey through each day had also become routine unless interrupted by an interrogation. As Grif had said, "a good day was just seeing these four walls." I guess I had made some kind of psychological transition; I now treasured the peacefulness of solitude, of just being left alone to pray and sing to myself. Every new mark on my calendar meant another day in God's plan and another day closer to our return.

My heightened sensitivity to light and my acute sense of hearing over smell and touch was a mixed blessing. I despised the intrusion of the wall light and tried to remove the cover to unscrew the bulb. From outside, the irritating sound of the diesel generator was annoying. The guards' radio was too loud and although I was frustrated that I couldn't understand Arabic, the longer I listened the more I thought I understood. Several times a day Saddam's voice would fill the air with some kind of propaganda speech. Every now and then though, I would hear a familiar jingle like the *Bonanza* theme song associated with a commercial. It was a note from home— a little bit of America.

Another frustration with being so close to the guards' table was being able to hear them stir their tea in the morning and rustle around in a paper bag of bread. Then at night the clatter of their knife and fork during their evening meal was a tormenting reminder that we weren't eating. The first few days if I knocked on my door to ask for water a guard would infrequently answer, "Who is it?" I would answer, "26, MAI-ah." (Coming back once I caught a glimpse of my cell number. It was the same as the old jail.) The curt reply was always predictable. "Five minutes." It was soon easy to recognize the different guard's footsteps and voices; their dress was as different as their demeanor. A couple wore para-military garb; others dressed in business suits with white shirts and ties, and one or two in traditional Arab robe and headdress. Only a few would come to the door; only two would give me a drink. The only regularity was a meager feeding early afternoon and some kind of head count taken about every other day. One day when one of the more tolerant guards looked in, I asked about food. He said, "You eat at two o'clock." Of course I didn't have a watch and he wouldn't tell me what time it was.

Tuesday, February 5th

The gray light of morning never found its focus on my wall nor did the dismal clouds let through any golden tones. The dreariness only seemed to get worse. As I marked my calendar I was already weary of the waning moon and the glint of light it was providing to soften the insanity of the night.

Late morning I could hear flapping on the outside of the building. Risking being caught again, I scrambled onto the divider and watched in horror as a tarp was lowered outside over the window—my precious light was nearly choked off—my world was being closed in. For a moment I felt as if I was suffocating.

After noon I heard the pipes gurgling and realized our meager water supply had been turned off. The war was coming home to my cell. The only thing running with any frequency was that annoying generator.

That evening in the dark I continued to pace although my rectangular course was now more of a staggered circle. I was too upset to lie down; I knew it was early—a couple hours till air raid show time. The imposing tarp had altered my sense of time.

After so many days of trying to focus on just staying alive and being positive, I began to think about my family. Somebody, probably Jumbo, had to notify Barbara that I didn't come back from that mission on the 19th. The whole scene started to play out in my mind's eye. Both in Goldsboro and at my mother and stepfather's in Brazil, Indiana, the dreaded blue-car-in-the-driveway and uniformed personnel at the door. It hit me hard.

I imagined Barbara in the kitchen. Instead of some official notification parade, I saw Jumbo and Nancy walk over from their home across the street and knock on the kitchen carport door. I thought he'd have his flightsuit on—not a blue uniform. Barbara would let them in but then would probably see the seriousness in Jumbo's eyes and start backing up, her emotions erupting. I knew as strong as she was it would be really tough. I cried for her and tried to imagine holding her in my arms. If this had to happen, I was glad Jumbo and Nancy were there. They would hold her, too.

In Brazil, I imagined the blue car driving up the long driveway. Bill, my stepfather, not expecting company that late, would go to the door. Then he would call to my mother. She would listen to the Air Force representatives but I felt she might not accept what they were saying. Instead, she would turn to God and put my future in His hands. I knew the power of her prayers and while I cried that night I knew I was just crying out of my own uncertainty for the future.

Since it was a Saturday night, Timm might not be home when Jumbo came over but he would see any lingering visitors when he came in later. I wasn't sure how he would take the news; he was strong-willed and seemed to share an inner faith despite his own search for identity. I recalled our visit in early August, just days before my deployment, to the UNCW campus where he was to start college in Wilmington. After I deployed, Barbara wrote that he had expressed his own desire to "join up" but she had insisted he go on to college and moved him in for freshman orientation. By mid October, however, he had become so preoccupied with Desert Shield that he returned home to Goldsboro. My promise on leaving that I'd "be back for parents weekend" in September was as naïve as my belief that we'd ever go to war. As I tried to bring my emotions together while I continued to pace in the darkness I wondered if my situation was meant to foster a new level of maturity in his life.

Emotionally drained, I eventually balled up on the floor to sleep. I knew I had to stop thinking about the situation at home. Beyond praying for their comfort there was nothing I could do. I needed to stay alive and stay focused. For now I was coping.

February 6th

It had been a tough night. Waking once, I made the mistake of opening my eyes to see if it was morning. Whatever was hanging on the outside of the building had blocked even a glint of the remaining quarter moon. In the silent void where the hard floor was the only dimension, my mind's eye had begun to tumble my senses. I quickly closed my eyes in panicked desperation and placed my bare hand out flat against the cold floor to anchor my boundless world. I realized I had to keep my eyes closed in the dark so they would not struggle to find light. This way the dimensions of space in my cell were relative to my daylight perspective and I didn't get mentally lost in the dark.

Water was a problem again. It was useless to ask, it only brought disappointment and served as an opportunity to be harassed by the guards. The immediate problem however was the cold. The solution was to block the air coming through the vent but it was too high to reach. So, every time they cranked up the generator it got colder.

This helplessness and frustration brought an end to any polishing of my release speech. I knew the main points must be to thank God for bringing us home, to thank anyone gathered to meet us for their support, and to highlight the ideals of freedom. I figured there would be plenty of time to fine-tune it when we were told we were to be released. Besides, I was more interested in getting back to Al Kharj even though I was starting to think that maybe I would need a few days to get my strength back.

Without interruption, my regimen of praying and recalling hymns while pacing had become the core of my waking moments. I also recalled stories from my association with
some of the Viet Nam returnees as they came through Randolph
AFB during my assignment in 1973. As isolated prisoners,
they had constructed houses, recalled even minute details of
novels, and stretched their minds beyond imagination during
their captivity. For me, I began to reconstruct the details of
family outings and trips, recall life acquaintances and work
experiences, and walk the streets of Brazil imagining friendly
faces and greeting old friends. It was a simple, although sometimes emotional way to pass the time and kept my mind from
dwelling on my stomach, the cold, or the unknown.

With the dark came the waiting. Would tonight's attack be closer? Certainly the Saudis had informed the allies
where we were. Whether we were rescued or just waited it out
was far beyond my control. Often at night I would recall our
church youth group dismissal: "May the Lord bless you and
keep you. May the Lord lift up his countenance before you
and give you peace." Other nights, as I pulled my body into a
fetal position, I would simply pray the prayer of my childhood: *Now I lay me down to sleep, I pray the Lord my soul to
keep.*

Thursday, the 7ᵗʰ
    *Good morning Lord, and Lord it is a good morning. Re-
gardless of where I am I know you are with me and, I am still
alive. Please give me the strength and courage to survive today.*

By the time the light bars had reached the floor (maybe
mid-morning), I sensed a change to the guards' routine—something was going on at their post. There had been some cell

door activity and I could hear some limited English and an infrequent two-beat muffled tapping. There was no slapping around, no loud threats, no chairs being slammed. I couldn't figure it out.

A short time later someone came my way and unlocked my door without first looking in. "Come," he said as he motioned his hand around his chin. "Clean." It was apparent he wanted me to go with him to shave. Man, just what I don't need. Here we are trying to live in this icebox and he wants me to get rid of my face blanket. No way! "No, SHOOK-ran," I said and made a shivering motion. He slammed the door and went back to the left. From his tone of voice, I could hear my decision was not popular. And, as I quickly thought about it, he didn't have a blindfold or cuffs. Maybe this would give me a chance to check out the hallway and the guards' station.

Within minutes one of the bad guards came back with a look of determined vengeance. I went.

From my cowered glance this was a no-kidding prison. The big steel doors looked even more foreboding from the outside. Down the forlorn hallway there were at least eight cells on each side, to my right, maybe half a dozen. Across from the only window and the elevator at the center point of the corridor was the guards' hangout. I had imagined correctly that I was just one cell off the middle and diagonal from them.

Quickly, I was pushed to the back of the desk area where they had laid out a pair of scissors, a couple double-edge razors and three or four disposable Bics. There was also a small mirror, the remains of a whisker-covered small bar of soap, and a dirty coffee cup of used shaving water. After pointing to "sit," the guard motioned again for me to shave.

Except for the eyes, I barely recognized the stranger's face I saw in the mirror; I had grown a fairly respectable beard. Shaving was not going to be easy. I dipped the soap in the water and rubbed it on my mustache. Picking the cleanest of the razors I started to tug on the whiskers. It was useless. "MAI-ah, more water?" I asked. The guard picked up the cup, threw the remains on the floor, and then scooped the cup in a bucket. "Now, quickly," he said. Again I started but without any real lather I might as well be using a wood plane. Still, it was not going well, or least fast enough, so the guard took another razor and knocked my hand away as he grabbed the back of my hair and scraped into the left side of my face. I winced as he torn into my chin; the blood started dripping on the old wet newspaper on the desktop.

"OK, OK," I said and began again to slowly whittle away at three weeks of growth. By the time I finished I looked like a sprinkling can with dripping cuts all over my face. The guard was trying to stop the bleeding by wiping my face with an old rag and then just tore off pieces of soggy newsprint from the table and stuck it to my cuts. God, what a mess! As he pulled on my arm to go I saw another bucket of cleaner water by the wall and leaned over to splash my face. Back in my cell I thought about the bloody newspaper pieces I had left floating in their drinking bucket.

A little bit later another guy holding a blindfold opened my door. By my senses it was getting close to feeding time but I had no choice but to go. He bundled me up and then took my forearm and led me out to the elevator. Passing the guards' post I wanted to tell them to just keep my lunch in the micro-wave. I was surprised that I wasn't handcuffed but didn't think much more about it. I did put one hand softly on the top of his hand to make human contact and steady my walk as I had done with Ali. In the small elevator we went down to the first floor and then walked toward the back of the building. Once through a doorway, we stopped. I could hear the door close and then someone removed my blindfold.

I was in a small auditorium. There were some theater-type seats with about six to eight men standing around. The focus of activity was a television interview set—two chairs with a small table in between and a coffee table and radiant heater in front. I was directed to pick through a pile of flight suits and put one on. (I found the biggest, most ill-fitting I could.) Then they sat me down in the chair to the left as someone tried to brush my hair and then pick a piece of bloody newspaper from my face.

Slumped forward, I shivered as I leaned toward the heater. What I had learned since August from my association with my new Arab friends in Oman, Air Commodore Ahmad al-Rawwas and Colonel Mohammed, was that arrogance has no place in the Arab world. This definitely applied in dealing with an Arab enemy. The ugly American syndrome when applied to a resistance situation could get a guy blown away in a Baghdad second. There was a time to be bold, proud and a defender of freedom and a time to be frail, quiet, and humble. This was not the time to rehash the morality of their invasion of Kuwait.

A clean-cut man in a gray pinstriped suit with a white shirt and red tie sat down to my left and began talking to me in lightly accented English. He said he was going to ask me some questions and that he expected me to answer correctly. Someone else beside the camera started directing the whole thing while the interviewer kept telling another to wipe my face. "Sit back," (from the heater) he said. Then, just before he started, a glass of water was placed on the table.

He started talking into the camera and, with unsteady hands, I picked up the glass and drank all the water. This stopped the shot while they refilled the glass and I moved back toward the heater. With the glass reset, we started over—him talking, me drinking, then shivering, and all the time bleeding. Again they reset, now with the heater pushed up near my legs and another glass of water on the table. I drank the water again. This time they didn't replace the glass. Still, we soon got to the point were they wanted me to make a political statement about how the war was wrong and that American pilots should not bomb the people of Iraq. I guess I had too much trouble following his English because I was always giving the wrong answer. Fortunately, there were too many other people around for any adjustment of my attitude and they finally just dismissed me. Off the set, I took off the flightsuit and then downed another glass of water before someone put a blindfold on me and grabbed me by the sleeve. Strangely, I'd had enough socializing for the day and was eager to get back home—to the solitude within my four walls.

Back in my cell I was pleased my bowl had been partially filled. Unfortunately, the cold had coagulated the grease on top. But it just didn't matter—it was food. I sorely remember guzzling half of it down before I realized I hadn't thanked God; I broke into tears.

Sometime later the water came back on and then before dark the tarp that had been covering the window was pulled up allowing more light to come in. It was answered prayer and a reminder to *wait upon the Lord.*

That evening I added another hymn lyric to my list:
"Count your many blessings,
Count your many blessings, name them one by one.
Count your many blessings, see what God hath done."

Four more days

Locked away where daylight and darkness seem to be just another part of an endless nightmare, change can be as significant as a sneeze in the hallway or the slam of a vehicle door outside. Time is measured in moments; some moments are a lifetime. Nothing was done on my schedule and my own worst enemy was self-pity, anxiety, and impatience. Living had taken on a whole new meaning.

Beyond the incredulous threat of having my head blown away, I had in my mind worked through the scenarios for being publicly executed several times. The news video of President Nicolae Ceausescu and his wife facing a firing squad in Romania and the hanging corpse of Marine LtCol Higgins assigned with the UN in the Sinai were still vivid in my mind. I felt with God's help I could get through either of these death sentences. I was concerned, however, about being stoned by already provoked citizens and played out that Biblical scene more than once.

I was doing my best to keep my legs limber and I continued to pray, pace and exercise my mind through thought travel. Instinctively, however, my senses were always keen to any potentially threatening activity of the guards just outside my cell door. Over the days and nights I had produced my own travelogues and would selectively visit them like adventures at a theme park. I was captive in this cell but my mind was still free.

Here are some of the sequels of my sanity:

My family. After my emotional crash the night of the fifth, I was cautious in allowing my thoughts to venture home to be with Barbara. Our last minutes together that Thursday morning seemed like a hundred years ago. I think we both shared the excitement of the deployment and the naiveté that it would be like all the others to Zaragoza, Spain or Deccimomano, Sardinia—just a couple weeks. Still her parting words reflected her insight into the seriousness of the world crisis: "You've trained twenty years for this. . . ."

We had been deployed to the Gulf region long enough that I knew our friends and the base support system were taking care of the house and yard, so I tried to focus memories. It was comforting to recall previous assignments, places where we had lived, friends we had made, and our vacation trips throughout Europe. Deep in thought, I retraced our steps together through the seventeen moves of our Air Force journey. We both shared an abiding trust in God and an unspoken faith in His plan. This was not a test; it was just life. From my perspective my life was in his hand—in the hand of the one who calms the sea. Likewise, at home in Goldsboro, Barbara and Timm were under His wing.

My hometown. When you grow up in a town of 8,000 people, deliver daily newspapers, work in a men's clothing store and play golf beginning at age seven, you know a lot of people. I could spend hours as I paced round and round, visualizing in my mind walking the streets of Brazil, Indiana, and recalling faces and experiences with old friends, acquaintances, and classmates. Now this part of my early life seemed as close as if it was yesterday. Riding my imaginary bike down the streets, I could see the houses along my paper routes and I tried to remember who took the *Daily Times* and who also took the Indianapolis paper. My reminiscence of working for Jack at Leifheit Men's Wear was filled with special memories. Sitting there day dreaming of our times doing inventory I finally figured out why he put the letters "MT" on certain boxes on the top shelves. And then, the excitement when Bill, a more senior salesman, would propose a coin-flipping game of "king bee" for the afternoon lemonade. A special part of my hometown was our park—Forest Park. Oh, the fond times I spent growing up there in the cool shade of her trees, enjoying the giant double slide, and swimming at the pool. With great emotion, I remembered the night my Dad, sitting in a wheelchair, participated in my Bobcat Scout ceremony in one of the shelters.

I owe a lot to the acquaintances I made beginning at age seven at the golf course. As the legendary Harvey Penick said: ". . .and if you play golf, you're my friend." I was truly blessed with a lot of role models, from dentists and doctors to car dealers, newspapermen, business professionals and neighbors. My mind replayed every one of those nine holes from drive to iron to putt. Ironically, our high school class had just held its 25th reunion in the summer before we deployed. As I tried to recall all their faces alphabetically I wondered if any one would ever hear that I didn't make it back that night. As if I'd never see some again, I was glad I had taken time to write before the war. Brazil had its share of Viet Nam casualties— one, a pilot, Brent, whom I always admired. At his funeral the minister said he had died to preserve our freedom—lost words at the time. Teachers readily came to mind also. Sitting there in the dark, I wondered if any of them would ever know what happened to me. Only at certain times could I ever take my thoughts home to Brazil and just sit in the kitchen and watch my mother as she went about her day. Some time travel was more difficult than others.

Life in the Delt House and the Indiana campus. What great memories I had to relive from my college years. By choice I had lived all four years in the Delt House. While it provided the academic discipline I needed to survive, it was also filled with unimaginable episodes only hinted at in the movies. Those days in the House with Jim Marshall, Huck and the bros were a hundred years ago. Pledgeship, blanket parties, serenades, the annual Luau and always "me and my gal from Delta town." Barbara and I had shared some wonderful times on the I.U. campus in Bloomington. Walking through the leaves in the fall, making snow angels in the winter, and then spring afternoon trips to Brown County State Park. Those were the real wonder years!

Disney World. In May of 1987, we had gathered with Barbara's Uncle Ed and his family for several days at Disney World. I spent hours imagining our drive along I-95, the hotel where we stayed and our time in the different sections in the park. During the visit we had celebrated my birthday with an evening dinner while, on the restaurant television, the Celtics and Larry Byrd battled for the NBA championship. Part of the construction in the park was the new Floridian Hotel complex. Although we had only viewed it from the monorail, I tried to imagine the pastel colors and visualize its completion. In my mind I pretended to walk around the pool area and imagine the families laughing and playing together. When we get home, I told myself, I'll try to live the dream.

Marathons. I loved to run. Taking two steps, turning, taking three steps, turning, and continuing the rectangle was a different pace than the eight-minute miles of my normal run. Still it was therapeutic exercise, and it helped me keep warm. I would imagine running from the Athletic Club at the Pentagon, across the Memorial Bridge, past the Lincoln and Washington Monuments, along the mall and around the Capital. Coming back across the bridge, I'd always pass this long striding guy who'd throw a big air five to all the runners. I relived the mileposts along the C &O Canal where Bob Stocks and I trained together for the Marine Marathon. Other times, I would try to retrace the track of the New York City Marathon and would relish the encouraging cheers of the crowd at the U-turn off the Queens Bridge and then along the final three hundred yards in Central Park.

Canoeing the James. During my second tour at the Pentagon, two of my fellow Air Force buds and I bought Mad River Canoes to take our teenage sons and daughters on weekend canoe trips during the summer. We had started on the Shenandoah and progressed to the Rapidan and Rappahannack Rivers before settling on a magnificent section of the James. With the help of The James River Runners, we would put in at Howardsville, fish and camp along the way, and then finish at the Hatten Ferry. What great times to relive. Pacing around I would methodically pack all our gear, sort through my tackle box, and load my canoe before imagining the drive down Highway 29 to Charlottesville for breakfast at McDonalds and then on to Scottsville. Along the river, I would rock in the rapids and visit the fishing spots while remembering how it was to float along in the hot sun. There were no real campgrounds but we did have a special island where we'd try to camp. I'd go through the whole adventure: pitching the tent, collecting firewood, cooking dinner and breakfast, and trying to catch the first fish of the morning. If only Timm or Larry, Joe, and I could go one more time.

My other escape involved transitioning my perspective from looking at my scratching on the opposite wall or just staring at the light in the high grated windows to an out-of-body experience looking at myself from above as I sat against the wall in the cell. Expanding my imagination further, I would try to visualize the rows of cells, then the building, the city, the country, and even the Earth from a distance. Depending on how patient I was in shifting my perspective, I created more and more detailed definitions to each scene.

Tuesday, the 12th

I had been praying a lot about our diet, too. Besides not getting enough water, we were getting no protein or sugar and very little carbohydrates. I really resented the sound of the guards stirring sugar into their hot tea in the morning and longed for a hot cup of sweet black tea from the old jail. Sometimes I had found myself dreaming about the sweet dates and tea the Air Commodore had offered me in our first meeting upon our arrival at Thumrait on the 10th of August. Those months in southern Oman had been challenging and full of opportunity. I wondered if Rowwas would fondly remember me someday.

That night I had already fallen asleep after the routine night attack when a relatively new guard, also wearing a red and white ghutra, startled me by opening my feeding door. Suspiciously, I expected another pointless late night interrogation but instead he motioned me to come closer. He put his hand up to the space and handed me five dates. I was awestruck. Quickly, to show my appreciation, I ate one. Then he asked if I wanted any water. I couldn't believe it. He poured me a drink and "water again." Now I shivered and asked for a "Blanket SHOOK-ran." He stepped away leaving the little door open and shortly returned to open my main door and hand me a blanket. Before he closed the door, I touched my chest and said, "David." He mirrored my action and said, "Abas." As he closed my door, I said, "God bless you, Abas." He was like an angel.

Stingily, I put the other four dates in the top of my sock and thanked God for all His blessings. The extra blanket meant I could triple fold one to lay on and still roll up in another. In my mind I could again hear the cheers of Lawrence as he headed for Aqaba. I too, knew that with God's help through men like Abas, we could make it.

The 13th

I slept well; the added blanket on the cold concrete floor was like sleeping on a cloud and from the beam of light against the brick I could tell it was a cheery day outside. In contrast, the caustic voice I recognized in the hallway was of the worst of the guards. I hoped he would just leave me alone until feeding time. I had a lot to do today and certainly didn't need to be bothered with his badgering. First, I had to decide about the dates. Should I eat the other four now or save them and risk having them confiscated. I compromised; I would eat one and put the other three back in my sock with the plan to eat one each of the next three days except Saturday. I would skip a day and save the last date for Sunday. As for eating a date, I didn't want any of it to be wasted so I just parked it on top of my tongue and let it dissolve. Then as the fruit came apart I would swallow the tiny bits of the skin. Eating a date could last for several hundred laps.

My other big project was to very quietly tear the silk edge binding off my blanket. I needed shoe laces and something for my waist to hold up my pants. The remaining strips I used to wind between my toes and to wrap my feet and ankles. All the walking had made them stronger but I could still see the remains of the bruising from the sprains. If we did get rescued there would be no slowing down for me.

The interrogations had become less frequent; the isolation more intense. Strangely, the mental challenges of the psychic battle of wills and endurance were refreshing yet somehow macabre. My desire for conversation did not, however, out-weigh the physical abuse aspect of the handicapped jousts with the enemy. Comparatively harmless, I found the constant noise of the radio and the unpredictability of the guards unconsciously kept my mind sharp. I yearned for the sound of the feeding cart. As the wobbly cart started down the hall towards my cell, I could hear the little doors opening and then being slammed. Some guys must have been asleep because the guard would yell at them as to say "Get up" or "Give me your bowl."

As weak as I sometimes felt, I would not let myself sleep or even lay down during the day. By walking I kept warm and then fell asleep at night before getting too cold. When I was sleeping I didn't know I was cold. At home when you wake slightly and feel a chill you can pull up the covers or close the window. In prison, you can't do anything but ball up tighter or get up and walk in a circle. Your dreams are always better than reality, too—the bad dreams start when you wake up.

Thursday, the 14ᵗʰ—the middle of February

Among my other waking thoughts and always greeting the day with saying *Good Morning, Lord,* I would anxiously look up to the window and stare at the light. The verse: *I will lift up my eyes unto the hills from hence comes my help* seemed synonymous to the importance I placed on the light. I knew God was always with me but I drew my strength from His promise: *I am the light of the world and who so ever believes in me shall not perish.* I imagined the rows of bricks as rungs on a ladder to the light—Jacob's ladder—and recalled the lyrics *We are climbing Jacob's ladder, soldiers of the cross.*

I couldn't remember all the words or verses of all the hymns that kept flowing through my mind but I would repeat first lines or choruses over and over. Until now I had just dwelled on a song as it randomly came to mind. Staring at the opposite sidewall I saw there was a two- by three-foot clean space to the left of my calendar. Among all the dismal scratchings and tallies on the wall, this was a perfect place for a list of hymns. I decided to add a witness that a Christian had done time here—*they will know us by our deeds, by our deeds…* Beginning with "A," I scratched the alphabet vertically; two letters to a brick and then began to record my songs starting with *Amazing Grace.* For some letters, I had more than one phrase.

A *Amazing Grace…, Are yea able…,* and *Amen*
B *Blessed Assurance…, Bless be the tie that binds*
C *Count your many blessings*
D *Do Lord, Do Lord, Oh do remember me*
E *Everlasting Arms…, Every time I feel the Spirit*
F *Faith of our Fathers…*
G *Go tell it on the mountain…, Glory, glory, glory*

H *How Great Thou Art…, Holly, Holy, Holy…, He lives, he lives*

I *It's me, it's me, it's me Oh Lord*

J *Just as I am…, Joy, joy, joy*

K *Keep me nearer, nearer, nearer Lord to thee*

L *Lean on me…*

M *My faith looks up to thee…, Mine eyes have seen the glory…*

N *Nearer my God to thee…*

O *Onward Christian Soldiers…, Old Rugged Cross*

P *Praise God from whom all blessings flow…*

Q *Q…*

R *Rock of Ages…*

S *Savior like a shepherd lead us…*

T *Take time to be holy…*

U *Up from the grave he arose…*

V *V…*

W *What a friend we have in Jesus…*

X *Christmas songs: Away in the Manger…*

Praise Yea the Lord, hallelujah

Z *Zion, Zion, we're marching onward to Zion*

By the time I finished, my fingers and hand hurt from working with the tiny drain screw. But there it was, certainly no Ten Commandments on a stone tablet yet still a somewhat bold testament to the secret of my sanity. Regardless of any attention my addition to the wall might draw, it was done and I felt good about it. At the bottom, I scratched my name: Colonel David William Eberly USAF 2/1/91

If we took another hit, maybe it would survive and someday our intel would know I was here. I can't remember if

I even thought about it being Valentine's Day. The only hint to human kindness had been Abas' sharing of some dates. He was special.

The night of the 15ᵗʰ

Sometime after the night attack I was rousted for another trip down the hall. Generally these interrogations took place in a little room at the far end on the left just across from the back stairwell. I was always blindfolded except for the trip out to shave. These sessions seemed like more harassment than anything else. At least as far as I was concerned we had long since run out of anything to talk about. The outcome of the game would be the same; the challenge was staying cool inside and simply making the right moves. Outwardly frustrated with their persistence to discuss Schwarzkopf's ground attack plan, my replies were always the same, "I just don't know! We were isolated from any integrated planning and as a pilot I was only given a pre-loaded cassette to fly—nothing more."

I don't remember the topic of the evening but at the end I asked if I could ask a question. Although unfamiliar with Ramadan, I knew it had special meaning to all Arabs and that if the war dragged on there might be a chance for release during that observance.

"When is Ramadan?" I asked.

"Why you want to know this?

"I know it is a special time and felt it might be close."

"No, not for another month."

"You mean the 15ᵗʰ of March?"

"No, 17ᵗʰ of March," he replied.

"SHOOK-ran," I said.

This time instead of being jerked up by my collar the

man behind me lifted my arm. Walking back down the hall I sensed my question might have briefly reminded him I was a human.

As always I finished my day with my own adaptation of the Lord's Prayer: *Our Father who is here with us. Thank you for this day and the food. Give us the mental courage and physical strength to get through the moment and please give them the courage to treat us fairly. Thy Kingdom come; thy will be done. For you are the real power and glory for ever. Amen.*

Saturday, the 16th

Another day that the Lord made. Let us rejoice and be glad in it.

The sometimes-good thing about Saturday was the weekend help. Frequently, whether out of curiosity or just boredom, a new guard would open the little door and look in on me. This could mean a drink of water or, during feeding, a chance for "soup again" (an extra ladle in the bowl).

I was not really optimistic about any release before the end of the war and at this point couldn't understand what was taking so long for our forces to roll into Baghdad. The good news from my isolated world inside the cell was that we were past the new moon. This meant that the night sky would be getting lighter over the next two weeks. And, with each passing day toward spring, the days would be longer—that meant the sun would be warmer. At some point we had to hit a happy medium when it wouldn't be so cold in this place. The cold was tough but I imagined the heat of the summer in these cells would be stifling and, without water, we wouldn't last long. For now we could get by on the bowl of tomato-based soup and frequent portion of bread but without a more reliable watering system, we'd be in serious trouble with the heat.

All this uncertainty could drive a sane man to panic. Through prayer my own frustration and anxiety seemed to have reached a level of inner composure that kept me focused on the moment. I had accepted death and put my hand in His. My responsibility was to stay alert, stay limber, and trust in God's plan.

Sunday.

I savored my last date as though it was part of a communion service. This place was a lifetime from our chapel at Seymour and another hundred years from Epworth. Still, I tried to sit along side Barbara and Timm as I pretended to join in the service. With Chaplains Ray and Jim deployed with our folks at Al Kharj, Stu would be leading the worship. Back in Brazil, the center of my attention had always been the large brown chalk portrait of Jesus over the altar. From a pew I could see my mother holding her place in the choir as the last note of "How Great Thou Art" underscored the congregation's abiding faith. My link to both was those hymns now scrawled on my wall.

That night, after the all-clear siren, I followed my routine and may have already fallen asleep when I heard some nearby doors slamming in sequence. There were no shuffling sounds, no commands. Then footsteps came to my door. My little door opened and I sensed the dim wall light was on so I uncovered my head and started to get up. It was always a dilemma whether to get up or not. When someone opened the door slot I didn't want to miss a chance for water or more dates. Sometimes the intruder just stared as though he was doing a college room check in case we might have gone out for dinner and a movie. "Sit down!" he yelled. I got up anyway.

There stood one of the civilian guards, a relatively new guy with someone else standing by his left shoulder. The figure was tall and dressed in a black monk-type robe with the shawl pulled up over his head. I couldn't see any of his facial features. They both were motionless and silent until the guard finally spoke in broken English, "Where are you from?" Hesitantly, as always, I replied, "U.S." After another interminable pause the monk grunted, the guard closed the door, and they both moved on.

Monday night, the 18th

After another day of listening to the same off-key Arab tree-saw music interrupted with meaningless gibberish and Saddam's afternoon speech, I realized we were well into darkness and as yet no air raid siren. The silence was unnerving. I knew the bombing had to halt before we ever had a chance for release, but such thoughts where beyond the disciplined limits of my self-imposed imagination. Along the corridor I heard the sequence of viewing doors. I sat and waited. When my door opened, I stood. It was the same guard from last night but without the monk. Unbelievably, he asked if I needed water. Of course "Yes, please." He poured me half a bowl and watched as I finished it all. Sensing he was sympathetic, I said, "MAI-ah again, please." "Again?" This time he filled my bowl. As he closed my door I thanked him again.

The 19th

Sometime after noon but before feeding time I distinguished Abas' footsteps in the hallway. There hadn't been a lot of chatter from the guards' area this morning and now it seemed that he was making the rounds alone. In sequence he opened my door and handed me a bar of soap. Beyond belief, another answered prayer. Of course the water was still off, but it was worth dipping the bar in my drinking bowl. It had been almost a month since I had been able to wash my hands or around my mouth. After wetting the bar I rubbed it against my face and hands and raked my long fingernails across it; the smell was striking. (Early on I had lost my sense of smell.) Ripping off one of my pants back pockets I made a combination washcloth and tooth rag. How invigorating to wipe my face; what a blessing.

Late afternoon during one of Saddam's radio propaganda messages I thought I understood something in the Arab gibberish about "Russians" and a "bombing halt." Although there had frequently been reference to Ameriki President Bush, this time I was certain there was something also about Gorbachev.

Again that night there were no sirens and no AAA.

Wednesday, January 20th

The quiet of the last two nights heightened my awareness that our situation might be changing. I hadn't seen the dastardly maitre d' on shift lately, and with some apparently new guards on duty, we weren't doing too badly on water.

Without warning around noon, two guards opened my main door. This was apparently for no walk in the park as they were holding not only the routine blindfold but had taken the wrist chains off the handle outside my door. I put out my hands, but then after a brief exchange, the guards left my hands free. They led me down the hall but this time instead of turning left into the little room they guided me down the stairs and into a different, larger room. My host was extremely agitated. Considering the time relative to feeding I wanted to tell him to "get through it—I have a lunch reservation upstairs." Fortunately, I kept my mouth shut.

This was one of the toughest psychological interrogations ever. In addition, one of their favorite tricks was to try and ease around to my side and then smack the side of my head, trying to burst an eardrum. The secret was to concentrate intently on any movement and stay aware of the on coming swat, then slightly tilt my head to defeat a direct blow. Today, from my position on a straight wooden chair in the middle of the room, I was conscious of at least two bad guys and knew I would have to keep all my senses tuned.

Immediately he started yelling about "American bombing—killing women and children." Then the other man said they were trying to protect me from a guy in the next room whose daughter had been killed by an American pilot. They were "holding him back." He said I should know how he feels. How would I feel if strangers killed my wife—if someone bombed my home and killed my son? They were going to take me "downtown, into the street" and "let the (angry) people" deal with me. My mind quickly flashed to the stoning scenario and silently I prayed for courage. "If you must," I said quietly from behind the blindfold. Then he went on.

"We are winning," he said. "Soon you will see."

"70,000 US soldiers have been killed. We have 2,000 American prisoners like you in a camp south of the city. We will take you there to talk to them."

"Mubaruk (of Egypt) has been exposed as American CIA. Your President Bush has been shot—he's dead. Quayle is now in charge. You tell us now, will he use nuclear weapons?"

My reply was impassive yet soft spoken. "We will not lose this war."

This ignited the Iraqi to my right side. With some Arabic expletive he slam-cocked an automatic pistol he must have been holding and jammed the barrel against the side of my head. It all happened so quickly. My thoughts raced to *the valley of the shadow of death. . .thy will be done* as the primary interrogator smacked the table and yelled something in Arabic. Time stopped. Then, with emotions peaked he tried to trump my stoic response, "You must now write apologies to the families" of the women and children who were killed. Unfortunately, I was apparently overwhelmed by their threats and was having a difficult time keeping myself from choking from dry heaves. This prompted the first guy to pour me some water. My measured reply was something like: "It is sad that they and their families have suffered but you know we did not bomb them." Furious, one man left the room and slammed the door.

It was quiet but even blindfolded I could tell the first guy was still there. Finally, he began again. "OK, we give you one more chance. You are colonel, tell me the army attack plan."

Bewildered, I cocked my head as to acknowledge what he had said and then replied. "You mean it's the 19th of February (knowing it was the 20th) and the army hasn't attacked yet?"

"Yes," he said.

I had no reason to believe him. If he would lie about the date, he would lie about the rest. Slowly, I spoke again. "I have no idea," and showing great disappointment, I softly muttered, "I can't believe it's been a month and the army still hasn't moved."

He was not convinced. "You know the plan, you are a colonel. If you don't tell me you are going back up to that hell hole."

Now with that threat my mind flashed to the exchange between Briar Rabbit and Briar Fox when old Mr. Fox tells the poor rabbit in his grasp that if he doesn't cooperate he's going to throw him in the prickly briar patch. And, Briar Rabbit, beaming on the inside, shivers and says: "Oh please, whatever you do, don't throw me in the briar patch!"

Beaming on the inside, I remorsefully replied: "I just don't know; I'm only a pilot. I could make up something but I just don't know." With that, he yelled at someone else who jerked me out of the chair and then he said, "You go back and think."

Going up the back steps all I could think about was O' Briar Rabbit singing "Zippidy Doo Dah" as he bounced around as a free bunny in the sticker bushes. Now, safely inside my briar patch, I smiled as I recalled the rabbit's song. "My, oh my, what a wonderful day," I hummed as I slid down the wall to sit on my blanket. My food bowl was on the floor; the cold layer of grease coating the broth just didn't matter. Staring at my calendar while I swallowed the cold soup, I was again conscious of the number '43.'

That night, almost on schedule, the sirens' wail seemed louder than ever. The tracers from the AAA cadenced the ratcheting of the guns and the distant explosions signaled a renewed allied emphasis.

But the day ended on a stranger note. After the attack, I was awakened again, blindfolded and taken back down the hall, this time into the small room on the left where I sensed three men. Still blindfolded, I was told they were checking for sexually transmitted diseases and that I was to drop my trousers. Absolute terror filled my body, as lightening seemed to strike my nerves. I had read how the Iraqis had mutilated the Iranians. Could this be their response to my performance earlier today?

Slowly I fumbled with my knotted waist tie and then, holding my breath, lowered my pants. Their response was quick: "OK, finished." I had purposefully tried to hold in my stomach. From under my blindfold I could see the frightening bony structure of my pelvic area. I cinched my waist and faintly asked, "Are you a doctor?"

"Yes, why?" he replied.

"I've been asking to see a doctor for three weeks. I have a bad skin problem but I know some of the others are sick—please check."

"Yes, we'll see," he replied.

The 21ˢᵗ

Feeding time. Watching the guard dip into the bucket, my eyes were filled with awe at the bulk mixture in the ladle. And then, without my pleading, he made a second dip into my bowl. It was a banquet: thick tomato broth with chunks of meat and vegetables with rice and a whole piece of Arabic flat bread. God, I was famished.

About dusk I became conscious of the faint sound of someone sobbing. I held my breath as I strained to distinguish any English. It's either Arab or Italian I thought and it seemed to be coming from the right. I couldn't tell, but I did know the guards weren't going to put up with this. His cries got louder and then echoed down the hall. From inside my cell the apparent agony became unsettling. It was a haunting, annoying manifestation of my greatest fear—going mad. Maybe it was this same threshold of sanity, not claustrophobia, which I sometimes approached when waking in the black and silent void of night. It can't be just me; everyone must be close to the edge by now.

An agitated guard yelled back several times, but the cries continued. Then one, then another and then the third guard of the despised rowdy bunch of the early evening shift ran past my cell. I could hear them unlock his cell door. They pounced like attack dogs. First, just yelling at him. Then I heard the slaps to his head and the hits to his body—like fists to a punching bag. All the time, they yelled at him. His sobs turned to screams and their punches brought more painful cries. I felt so helpless; no one could help. Inside my heart was racing as I paced back and forth. God, help him. Please. I wanted to scream no, no, no! As they pounded him his crying turned to pleading. He kept saying "George Bush, Saddam Hussein," and something else in Arabic over and over. Then they dragged him into the hall, there was more scuffling. It sounded like they were kicking him. His chants were overcome by his horrific cries. It just went on and on. I tried to focus on the guards in my mind and pray for them. *Dear God, please give them compassion…give him peace.* Finally, there were only whimpers and then quiet. I could hear them drag him back into his cell and lock the door. Emotionally, I was exhausted, my body trembling.

Within minutes the air raid alarm began to wail and for the first time the guards reacted. Someone knocked over a chair as they ran down the hall. I could hear them scramble down the back stairs. The fragile balance of sanity within the place was cracking. These guys are like a gang that has just mugged some guy and are now fleeing at the sound of a police siren. We don't need these guys here dispensing street medicine—get a doc and get this guy out of here, I thought.

Friday, the 22nd

The horrors of the night had resolved to a quiet serenity as I lived on to another day. My *Good morning Lord* included the hope that somehow the madman had been taken out while we slept. The morning calm gave me an inner peace like the melody of the old Mills Brothers' song, "We Three." I too, was now "living in a memory" with " my echo, my shadow, and me."

Hope for another hearty bowl of gruel was dashed when the bucket on the wobbly cart yielded only a watery broth—today there was no bread. Still, I appreciatively thanked God and continued through my regimen of prayer and praise. A short time later the Arab-clad feeder appeared again. Caution aside, I approached the small door. Then, beyond my most improbable dreams, he pushed a plastic bag of six flat pizza-bread crusts through the opening. I was awe struck—another miracle. Considering the bounty, I convinced myself to eat an entire half piece before securing the bag out of view from the door.

Around dark the sobbing started again and quickly turned to the same chant including "George Bush" and "Saddam Hussein." A curt command from the guards' post answered the cry. It was like a bad dream, very upsetting and worse, the same gang had come on the desk. They must do something, I thought. *Please God, not again tonight.*

The sobs turned to an unfettered wail. The guy had broken down; he was emotionally gone. The guard gang blew up and rushed by to the poor man's cell. They wasted no time dragging him into the hall. Again the painful sounds of their brutal kicks echoed down the walls, transforming our prison into a chamber of horrors. As I paced back and forth the terror seemed to be getting closer. Either he was crawling my way or they were dragging him toward my door. I heard the clatter of chains and then it sounded like they were beating him. They wrapped the chain around my door handle. I tried to take deep breaths; my heart was pounding loudly. Frantically, I was pacing like the Dustin Hoffman character in *The Rainman*. *Please God, mercy,* I begged. Then among the yelling and crying the distinctively familiar sound of the cocking of an automatic pistol. I gasped. *Well God, maybe it would be better if they just kill him—thy will be done.*

Amidst the yelling someone opened my door. I was almost paralyzed. Oh God, what now? A paramilitary guy grabbed my arm. Behind him in the dim light I could see three casually dressed civilian guys standing over a bloody body. My guy pulled me quickly to the left and down the corridor. In the little room at the end there were two more guys, one sitting behind a small table with a clipboard. "What is your name and when were you shot down?"

"Colonel David William Eberly. January 19th."

That was it. He grunted and the other guy pulled me into the hall.

On the way back, I held his arm and put my right hand across on his. Approaching my open door I could see the almost lifeless guy lying on the floor as they continued to kick his head and chest. He had pulled into a fetal position so it was difficult for me to see his face but I could see his nose and mouth were bleeding. Quietly I whispered to my leader, "This is awful, you must help him. He's sick. Please take him to the hospital."

"Yes," he replied.

Finally the frenzy ended. I could only imagine he must have passed out or they gave him a shot because it got quiet and I could hear them drag him back to his cell.

Saturday, the 23rd

Watching the morning light move against the bricks I thanked God for another day. *And Lord, it will be a good day.* Today I could start the day with breakfast—some of that wonderful flat bread. At least for now I didn't have to save a half or quarter of the pancake-sized piece pita bread in case we didn't get fed the next day. By nibbling on the other half piece from last night for a couple hours, I was unaware that it was feeding time. Abas had followed the feeding guy with water and the surprise of rice under the tomato broth was another answered prayer. The routine watery soup we were getting once a day the past month was nothing like the bowl with rice we had begged downtown in the hallway that first few days. But then, it wasn't worth the physical and emotional aggravation either.

This morning I had faintly heard the sound of a woman's voice. Incredibly, it sounded like it was coming from the cell almost across from me. And, for several days it seemed like the guards had been sharing some of their food and speaking Arabic with another man—a man possibly in the same cell. Maybe they were feeding the Kuwaiti guy that was in the old jail. Anyway, if we somehow got the chance to escape, maybe he would know where we were and be able to help get us out of town.

So many unusual things had happened in the past couple days. The solitude of "just these four walls" had been penetrated by many unnerving events. Helplessly listening to the never-ending cries of someone gone mad had put renewed emphasis on the line between life and death and the unending challenge to control my own sanity. I knew I had to stay alert and yet it was so comforting to lose myself in my imaginary travel. Today was Saturday, their holy day. Maybe we would have a quiet day and the only outside noises would be their calls to prayer. My prayer was that the madman had recovered his senses and that we would not hear his torment again tonight.

Dusk turned to dark and almost on my biological queue the sirens began to echo outside. At the first note, just like last night, the guards ran. Now, while the initial warning faded away in the distance I felt a compelling urge to sit down against the sidewall. Unconsciously I began to pull my blanket-shawl over my head as I alerted to the distinct sound of a low flying airplane heading directly at us. I recalled the violence of the nearby explosion back on the 2nd and tensed for the strike. There was a crackling noise and then I felt as though I'd been suspended in mid air. We're hit!

Just to my left, outside where I had imagined a portal and the generator, the structure seemed to explode. The glass in the high narrow window blew out through the wire mesh and steel grate. My mouth felt like I'd taken a big bite of dirt; my lungs choked with the smell of burned air. I pulled my legs tighter and buried my face between my knees as the building swayed with loud cracking noises. I could hear and feel concrete crumbling and imagined that any second the ceiling was going to collapse on me or the floor was going to drop out from below. In the hallway there was screaming, "Get us out of here! Hey! Can anybody hear? Let us out!" I sat stunned, my mind racing. I had nowhere to go but I knew I couldn't panic. Maybe I should move against the steel door or the other wall. Oh God, I began, then my thoughts filled with *the valley of the shadow of death, I will fear no. . .* Kaboom! A second stunning explosion from the other end of the building. They can't get any closer, I thought. Are we going to die right here? I heard the ceiling in the hallway collapsing and from deep underneath the floor, pipes burst and water gushed. Over and over, I prayed: *Thy will be done Lord.*

More yelling in the hallway. I sat tight—frozen in a ball, hard-pressed against the wall. Another rocking explosion. This time seemingly on the backside of the building. I could feel the building recoiling from the new strike. Inside, it seemed as though the whole place was collapsing. More crashing from outside my door like chunks of ceiling and florescent bulbs being smashed. Guys were yelling—there was damage to the cells. From across the hall, I heard a woman screaming.

It's got to be a four ship of F-111s I thought. Surely, the last bomb would fall any second. Dear God, we've made it through three—it's up to you. The interval passed—no bomb. Still shaking, I got up and felt toward the door. It was dark as a tomb. The smoke and dust were choking my lungs. I felt the door and pushed. Nothing. I tried the viewing and feeding door. Nothing. Someone was in the hallway. Guys were yelling their names: "Lieutenant Larry Slade, US Navy." "Captain Storr," yelled another. "Jeff Storr, S-T-O-R-R." Then I heard the fourth airplane and yelled, "Incoming!" as I dived for the wall.

Another hit toward the back. I couldn't believe the floor and ceiling held. My mind was flooded with possibilities. I heard someone in the hall. A voice called out, "Who's in the hall?" Another yelled, "Is anybody out?" "I'm out. It's me, Zaun. I'm out in the hall, but it's a mess." Someone else screamed, "Get the keys!" I heard walking, walking on broken glass. I felt trapped and helpless. We need to get moving before the guards come back. Then I realized, maybe they were blown away in the hall. We need guns, we need someone who speaks Arabic, and we need a map. Maybe we can stop a bus. I pictured us frantically trying to get out of the city in the dark.

In the midst of Zaun crashing around in the hall, the yelling continued. Storr and Slade seemed to be in the middle to my left. They were relaying. I yelled, "Grif, are you OK?" "Yes," came the reply, "he's asking about you." Guys were giving their name and unit—it had gotten more orderly. I could hear someone trying to sort through the keys in the dark. From the distant end it sounded like someone else was out. I heard someone yell out a name and then heard

"...from CBS News." I couldn't believe it. "The Iraqis have the media here already."

"Get us out of here," someone pleaded. The reply was almost funny. "We're in a cell just like you."

About this time I heard several Arab-speaking men shouting to each other as they hurriedly approached the building from the front. Their footsteps crunched through the broken glass. "Here they come!" I yelled. "Knock it off!"

In the hallway, loud Arabic yelling, shoving. Zaun screamed, "Don't shoot!" I cringed hoping there would not be gunfire. Doors were being opened. There were prying noises;

I could hear them working their way down the hall. They've got to get us out of here, I thought. It's another bug out, but this time I'm going to be prepared. I stuck my bread bag in my shirt and grabbed my blanket. In the dark I felt for my water bowl and then tried to take a drink—it was coated with dust. Then I wrapped my blanket around my shoulders and stuffed the ends tightly in my pants waist. Ready, I stood to the left of the door. If they just open the door and start shooting, I'll be safe.

I heard them at my door; it was stuck. While they worked to pry it open I moved back by the ledge and sat down. There had been no gunshots, but it was time to be humble and non-threatening. For an instant I considered feigning to be dead from the blast. Then slowly, with loud screeching, the door opened and a black shape yelled, "Come!" I stood up; he grabbed my arm and pulled me out into the hall. In the dim light from two lanterns I saw the damage: the ceiling was mostly caved in and fixtures were hanging loosely. It was unbelievable—like a coal mine tunnel. I wasn't sure we were going to get out. One guy had me by the shirt behind the neck as we picked our way to the left toward a lantern by the guards' table. I prayed that we wouldn't stumble over their bodies. From the side someone tried to jerk my blanket away; I twisted and pulled away. My tucking held. My guide yanked me left toward the front elevator. No, I thought. The steps are on down the hall—this way. He pulled me harder. "Hurry, hurry, hurry!"

In the dim light I saw another stairway. The guard stopped, grabbed another guy and dragged us down the narrow stairs. I held his arm for balance. We were half falling as we ducked under the hanging pieces of ceiling and tried to avoid falling through missing steps or stumbling over debris.

The guard was crazed in a full panic. "It's OK, it's OK," I kept saying. "Slow down, it's OK." At the bottom of the first flight I patted his shoulder. "It's OK, we're coming. Go slow."

The first floor was trashed. There was no way out. My thoughts of breaking away were quickly dismissed. I've got to go with the flow and not risk getting shot—I still have no idea where we are—I have to stay with the others. Ahead, down the stairs, there was yelling—we continued.

The basement was flooded with at least six inches of water and there were broken pipes hanging everywhere. From the coal shaft it seemed like we'd been transported to a sinking submarine. I can't remember how we could see but as we sloshed along I thought we were surely going to be electrocuted. Ahead in the far corner there was a bright light. This must be a way out. Again, broken steps and then we were outside.

To my deprived eyes it was bright as noontime—nearly a full moon illuminated the rubble of the building behind us. There were armed men all around and so many prisoners; I thought we were only about twenty. Some guards were making hand-offs of men being pulled along while others were dragging guys apparently too weak to walk. I, too, was out of breath; my heart was pounding. "It's OK, it's OK. Slow down, careful, it's OK," I pleaded as we crossed a marble-like terrace behind the building. Our destination was a bus that was stopped along the tree-lined street in the distance.

CHAPTER 13

The Bus

This was not a VIP tour bus. I was pushed toward the door as two guys started whacking the backs of my legs with walking sticks to help me up the steps. I stumbled aboard and realized there were no seats. Instead, morbid figures sat stoically in the darkness along the sides with their knees pulled up and their heads hunkered down. Black eyes pierced the dark. To the left, a woman was crying. There was space to my right, so I scurried along the floor to avoid another blow to the head. A guard was in the aisle yelling and ripping guys' shirts up from the back to cover their heads. "Head down!" he screamed and then jerked my blanket over three of us. We were a pathetic, ghostly lot of souls.

Under the blanket, I leaned against the guy to my right. "I'm Eberly, who are you?" I said. He grunted, but I couldn't make out his name. When the guard passed again, I leaned to my left and said again, "I'm Eberly, who are you?" He responded: "Oh, no." As the guard passed by, I could only think the worst. "It must be another (F-15) E guy—someone who knows me. Even worse, now they will know I've been lying to them all this time."

I repeated my name again. This time he said something like, "I know who you are. I interviewed you twice before the war." Then he whispered his name, "Roberto Alvarez." He had been with Bob Simon and was part of the press pool that came to Al Kharj the day before the United Nations deadline of January 15. I cringed. Now the presence of the woman took on new meaning. If they got members of the pool, this must be Edie Lehrer from AP. Roberto assured me it was not and briefly told me the story of their capture.

He and two others from CBS working with Simon had gone up to the Kuwait-Iraq border where Simon had wanted to do a particular story. In the process they had strayed too far into Iraq and were detained. For them, the situation went from dumb, to bad, to worse. Roberto's summary comment was simply: "Next time he (Simon) wants to win the Pulitzer Prize, he can get his own damn pictures."

Suddenly, we heard the now familiar horrifying cries of the madman as he was dragged toward us and then thrown on the bus. I lifted the edge of the blanket to see if he was American. In the moonlight I could see he was Arab, maybe in his thirties, and was wearing only striped pajama bottoms. His face was swollen and bloody and his back was bleeding from many cuts. Two guards had pulled him by the arms from the front of the bus and now were kicking and beating him with rubber hoses, trying to make him be quiet. It was a horrible sight; the incensed guards were so enraged. I couldn't help but think that some guards had been killed in the bombing and that they were taking their anger out on this poor man. Around the sides we sat helpless, sorely afraid to rise up against these bullies. All I could do was pray for their mercy on him.

In the midst of this madness another guard pushed Zaun onto the bus and into the guys sitting in the back. That's when I recognized Simon, beard and all. He was sitting taller than those beside him and seemed to be a magnet for head smacks.

It was all beyond belief, such a brutal scene being played out inches away. Our stench of filth mixed with the smell of fresh blood. I tried to slow my breathing to control my anxiety, but as my heart pounded away I couldn't help but think what bizarre circumstances in this war had brought together our eclectic group.

With renewed rage, they dragged the madman's writhing body by his feet off the bus. At first, I thanked God for their mercy, thinking they would just leave him beside the street. We could hear his sobbing under one guard's hateful commands as they pulled him around to the back of the bus. Then, like a burst of rapid gunfire, there was the sound of a chain being threaded around the bumper. "Oh God, no," I pleaded half-out loud. The guard yelled at the driver; the bus lurched forward and continued to the end of the street before stopping. I heard the chain again and then two guards came on the bus carrying the madman by the arms and legs and dropped him motionless on the floor. Presumably, death had come aboard. In the dim light the corpse-like specter now lay silently at our feet. The bus moved on. *What now, dear God? I prayed again: Please give us the strength and courage to get through this moment.* Strangely now, as I prayed for calm, I felt momentarily secure being wedged in between Roberto and the other guy.

Clearing the tree-lined street, the bus wound its way through the city. The bright moon shown like a huge floodlight, illuminating the top stories of buildings. The swaying trees were so beautiful. How can we ever take such sights for granted, I thought. After a month of dismal isolation, I was awed by the three-dimensional outside world. Under the hum of the motor, Roberto and I continued to whisper as though the other was to carry out our last testament. At one point, one of the three guards who had gotten on the bus after the madman episode walked back down the aisle and leaned over to us. "You must be quiet," directed the familiar voice.

"Abas, is it you?" I said.

"Yes," he replied.

"I am glad that you are OK."

More quietly now, I told Roberto how Grif and I had been hit, tried to evade and then were subsequently captured on the Syrian border. We talked about our experiences in different prisons and then most importantly exchanged family information in case one of us didn't make it home. It was a fortuitous camaraderie, a photographer and a pilot on a vile and endless journey toward the unknown, now sharing epitaphs with a common ending: "Tell (her) I love her."

CHAPTER 14

Joliet

Somewhere, after travelling at highway speed through the dark countryside, we abruptly slowed and pulled off to the right on a side-angled road. Through the window across the aisle I saw a wall-sized mosaic tile mural of Saddam Hussein. The bus stopped shortly in front of a solid metal gate; to the left was a guard tower. What's in store for us next in the chamber of horrors on Mr. Moose's Wild Ride? I wondered. Then, after some Arabic exchanges, the large black gate swung open and the bus began to inch forward scraping the side mirrors on the narrow concrete entrance. Maybe it was the scars of torment we shared with the madman or maybe just the fear of another unknown prison, but I found the moment extraordinarily claustrophobic even considering my days in solitary confinement. We only moved forward another hundred yards or so and then stopped along side a frightfully high metal wall with a small entry door. The whole place seemed deserted and I could only imagine we were about to be locked up in a cold abandoned warehouse without food or water. The surreal sight reminded me of the old junkyard on west Jackson Street in Brazil—a place from where as a small boy I felt there would be no escape if I ever got locked inside.

When the bus door opened, two mysterious men in brown monk robes and leather sandals came aboard. Their tone was gentle in contrast to the two paramilitary heathens. In the commotion Roberto got Abas' attention and asked if the four of them (CBS guys) could be together. I wanted to stay with them too but I knew it would be difficult; they were civilians. Still, there was some kind of sorting going on as we were pulled from the bus and led through the small metal doorway. Under the moonlight, we went across a small courtyard then up a couple steps and through another door. Inside there was hollowness to the structure and I sensed a thousand pairs of eyes were watching us. Straight away I was pushed into a small cell with several others. We just stood there shoulder-to-shoulder for a moment and then started to whisper. I had only counted six of us including the Kuwaiti in the old jail and now we were eleven Americans. Then the door opened and two Arabs, one in a robe and the other in paramilitary garb, walked unabashedly in among us. Neither was armed but the guy in the camo jacket was holding a small paper bag. He said he was in charge and that we would be "staying here and must obey the rules." We quietly gave him a "Yes sir." I asked if he would take Zaun's handcuffs off and then I think I said something about food and water. A third guy by the door freed Zaun and then, as he walked out, the guy-in-charge handed one of us the bag. It was half filled with dates.

All this human interaction was exhilarating. Even in the dim light I could see all the cells were crowded. Must be a popular vacation spot, I thought humorously. At least the welcome is more civilized. We all sat down against the two side walls with our legs pulled up or zippered between the guys across from us and began to quietly exchange name, rank, unit, and shoot down information while we passed around the bag of dates.

Storr was sitting across from me and started first. Someone to my right (Fox) spoke up immediately and said something like: "Dale Storr? You're supposed to be dead. They thought you went in…your squadron had a memorial service. Your brother was shipped home and they had the funeral." Storr was speechless, his face white as a ghost as he hung his head in anguish.

Cliff Acree was among the next couple. He introduced his backseater Guy Hunter whose nickname was "Great White," in reference to his white hair. They were Marines flying the OV-10. It was Guy I'd seen come in on crutches around the corner to my left at the old jail.

When Jeff Zaun introduced himself, Fox quipped in again. "Hey, you're on the cover of *Newsweek*!" And then, I think he said something about all the backlash of bad publicity it generated for Saddam. It was difficult to see much in the dark but most of the swelling had gone down from his face. He told us about getting out of his cell earlier after the bombing, crawling out on a window ledge but then realizing there was no place to go. The fact that he was on the cover of a magazine rang in my mind like the song lyric, "on the cover of Rolling Stone."

Grif was in the corner opposite from me. When he got to the part about flying with me, Fox spoke up again. "You mean Colonel David Eberly—he's here?" "Yes," I said. "George Bob (his squadron commander who I'd known in Germany) said to say 'hi' if any of us ran into you," he retorted. I chuckled; it was like news from home. I guess I was most surprised that he would know I was MIA.

Then Grif went on to say that we had three SA-2s coming at us and were hit by the second one. This really got my attention. "Three?" I said. I couldn't believe it. Three SAMs! I had tried not to think about our shootdown because I had felt so badly that I hadn't defeated the one missile. Now Grif was saying there was more than one. Maybe I could accept those odds.

Larry Slade, who I'd seen that first day at the old jail told about getting hit in the F-14. Larry and his frontseater, Devon Jones, weren't able to get together after landing. He wasn't sure if Jones had been killed or rescued but did say that rescue forces had come in. That had been the SAR effort Grif and I heard on Monday, January 21st.

Then came Fox's turn. "Jeff Fox, Lieutenant Colonel, A-10s from Davis Monthan. New guy, shot down just two days ago…"

"Two days ago?" I interrupted. "What the hell's the holdup? Where's the army? What's going on?"

"Well," he said, "the day before, on the 19th, they were all massing along the border to the Southwest." This was depressing news.

Someone else wanted to know who won the superbowl. At first we decided to wait. Then he told us. I asked who the *TIME* man of the year was. He thought it was Bush. Then as he relayed his story of capture by the "cave men," we all chuckled. It was almost funny the way the described his radio conversation as the Iraqis closed in on him. The quiet laughter did us all some good.

In the dim light I recognized Berryman, the Marine who had been brought in during those early days at the old jail. He told us about getting hit in the Harrier and how the Bedouins had hit him across the leg with a metal rod after one question.

Tice, an F-16 guy, added his story of electrical torture with the truck battery.

I was last. I added little to Grif's story but did pull out my bag of bread to share.

We talked about the CBS guys and someone mentioned there were half a dozen Brits as well as Mohammed, the Kuwaiti, and Mauritzio, an Italian. They were on the bus and thought to be in the cell next to us. We were sitting almost on top of each other but we agreed it was better than isolation.

The news about the ground force was dreadfully disappointing. Still, a lot had happened. God had saved us during the bombing, we were all together for now and with all these other prisoners here there must be a better feeding system. I was optimistic that our situation had to get better. Emotionally, we could support each other. It was like the camaraderie of a squadron. We would be stronger together; for sure, with all of us in this small space we should be warmer. Now, there was nothing more to do. I pulled my legs up tighter and rolled onto my side on an old piece of cardboard that was lying on the floor. As I finished the Lord's Prayer and was drifting off to sleep I heard Slade say: "What a way for the colonel to finish out."

Sunday, February 24th

The sound of cell doors opening and closing woke me. Lifting the blanket off my head I was stunned by how bright it was in the cell. As I sat up, my back and leg muscles reminded me of all the activity in last night's bug out. I could see the cut on Storr's forehead now; he had been the only one hurt in the bombing. The rest of us just looked like a bunch of street derelicts rounded up on a Saturday night.

What had initially seemed like an abandoned warehouse was actually a big-time prison somewhere in the country. We were in a concrete cell approximately six by eight feet on the first floor of an open two story cell block with a barred vice solid door. It was a setting right out the Blues Brothers; this must be Joliet. Each cell was packed with at least eight men who seemed to move only in an orchestrated pattern; their life's belongings hanging on a nail or rolled up with their pallet. Along the pitch of the roof there were large partially opened windows like skylights. I imagined the fresh air smelled wonderful—certainly the sky was spellbinding. One of the guys, maybe Fox, said he could see a cow in a field outside the small window at his end.

The people activity was captivating. There was so much going on in the cellblock. The other doors apparently weren't locked because on some signal, different groups would go to what was evidently a toilet area to our left. Then others would come out of the cells and go get a large bowl of food or pitcher of drink. Finally, one of the monks came to our cell and allowed us, two at a time, out to the toilet and then brought us a large jambalaya pan filled with a bean soup, some bread, and a pail of hot sweet tea. Since we'd left our bowls we just passed the pan and pail around and took turns. As I stared at the men across the way, I wondered how long some of them might have been there and if their families ever got to visit or send them necessities. Living like this, a guy would certainly share anything to make life easier. It's all relative, I thought. This is a country club compared to where we were downtown. Maybe we'll just stay here and let the monks take care of us. The food is great and we get to go to the bathroom.

By mid morning we had exchanged all our info when a paramilitary guard came to our door and directed us, "Come." I started out and then remembered to grab my blanket. He led us out the door into the small courtyard where there were several other guards and then motioned for us to spread out and sit down. We quickly learned this was not to be a day at the pool. With their hard plastic whacking poles they assisted us in sitting cross-legged, arms folded and bent at the waist to keep our heads down. To compound this torturous "no look" position, one of the guards threw my blanket over my head. This arduous position seemed like some form of Chinese torture and then as the sun beat down on me I began to have trouble getting enough air. Finally, I used the blanket as a tent and uncrossed my legs so I could grasp around my knees for support. To get my mind off the pain, I kept rearranging a handful of pebbles. It was obvious from the shuffling that others were moving around too, even at the risk of receiving corrections from the guards. And, it seemed like some guys were being taken out of the courtyard one at a time and then returned. I remember hearing a gunshot at one point and fearfully thought we might be in line to be shot. Certainly I didn't know where we were but I had hopes that sitting out in the open we might miraculously be seen on some overhead photography.

After what seemed like hours I decided to risk a break. "Toiletten," I said, seeing the feet of a guard nearby. It worked. He grabbed my hair through the blanket and pulled me up. Dropping the blanket, I followed his direction back into the cellblock to the toilet. It felt good just to stretch and move around. Finishing, I remember thinking about saying something to the guard like, I'll just go on back to the room now and take a nap. Right! Then, coming out, I made a bold move toward the shade and sat down near a bench against the sidewall to support my back. Besides, I could see that another guard had already thrown my blanket over someone else.

From this perspective I was able to get a better view of the courtyard. It was approximately thirty by sixty feet. The high metal wall with the small door we had come through the night before was to my left as I sat against our cellblock. Across from me was an identical, seemingly deserted building connected by a single story structure to my right, which completed the concrete horseshoe. Large, round metal washing tubs, brushes, and water hoses were strewn around the deck. Several blankets were hung on drying lines to the side. There was one gnarled old scrub tree next to the wall and, within copping reach, a small piece valuable piece of industrial sponge. I didn't see Simon or any other civilians.

Sometime after the sun had passed overhead three of the prisoners from inside came out and started washing some pans. We had clearly missed the feeding. So, when one of the paramilitary guards sat down on the bench near me I decided to cautiously ask for water. "May we have some water please, MAI-ah?" Disdainfully, he yelled to one of the monks who then brought around a pitcher and a cup to give the guys a drink. With that success, I thought. I would try to get us some bread. Again, he barked to one of the monks who then dragged around a gunnysack of hard rolls. Later, the guard on the bench asked where I lived. When I said Washington, he smiled, put his hand on his pistol. "Someday I will go to America and kill your family." I didn't say another word.

Without fanfare the word came. Some Arabic commands and then one of the guards grabbed a guy by the metal wall and got our attention. We were to follow in line behind. Out the door, a turn to the right and then quickly down the rock and grass road along the wall before we stepped inside the next entry door into a similar courtyard and cellblock. Here we were prodded up some steps and then put in separate cells off the right walkway: Grif in the first, me in the second, and Slade and the others on down the line. As the guard walked back by I tried to engage him for a blanket. "Five minutes," he said.

This was the smallest cell yet—maybe five by four feet. My pacing was reduced to a small circle. Besides some littered scrap cardboard it was just another cold and dismal concrete box bearing the agonizing hash marks of previous lonely hearts. There was an open concrete block for a window in the back wall overlooking the courtyard where we had spent the day but the view was mostly blocked by what looked like a steel highway guard rail. Fortunately the door was just bars, laced with pieces of plastic to stop the wind, and it allowed a wide view of the second and first levels of the block. Best of all, I could see the sky and, from a slightly withdrawn position, watch the comings and goings through the entry door.

By night it was apparent that not only were we not going to be fed but that there would be no trip to the toilet area. I was glad I still had the plastic bag with some bread. It was the bag that I needed most.

The day had been filled with continual activity. As I curled up on the cold floor I realized that I had let the events of the day captivate my thoughts. There had been so much to see. I had forgotten to pray; I had forgotten the Lord. Now in the dark, my emotions erupted as my soul asked for forgiveness and I prayed my Lord's Prayer. *...And Lord, it was a good day. And, thank you God, I don't have to listen to that incessant generator.*

Then, breaking through the stillness of the night, the distinct muffled wail of the madman lodged somewhere in the other building. He's still alive, I thought to myself. But they (the civilian prisoners) aren't going to put up with that.

The 25th

Had I not opened my eyes I could have imagined I was somewhere along the James on a fishing trip, the birds were chirping so loudly. There they were maybe six or eight on the walkway just outside my cell door pecking away for crumbs or bugs. I hastily reached into my shirt, tore off a piece of bread, and began to toss little crumbs through the bars. Hey, easy guys, we have to share, I thought. Now I realized how the famed Birdman of Alcatraz felt. What a joy to have such cheerful companions.

Noise in the courtyard drew my attention to the window. Through a small crack between the boards I could see the civilian prisoners from the other cellblock where we were the first night were already cleaning up from the morning feeding. Surely we'll get something to eat today.

Then a couple of the monks came into our block with some of that delicious bean soup mixture and black tea. Combined with some flat bread I had left it made quite a feast. Eventually, we got to follow the same ritual of going to the toilet area, which was around the walkway to the right (almost catty-cornered from me). This was my chance to empty my plastic bag in one of the open toilet spaces. There was no running water, just two buckets of water and a small piece of soap. While one was clearly set aside for washing hands, the other looked clear enough to drink with a cupped hand. Walking back I tried to distinguish the forlorned faces staring at me from inside the cells. I could see we were all suffering from the move. If only we could have stayed together in the other cellblock.

Back in the cell I realized I needed to redraw my calendar. As I scratched out a bar for the week and marked a 25 in the Tuesday space, I was again conscious of the number "43." Sadly, I realized that February had only three more days and then I would have to build a March square.

My mind was a jumble with frantic lines of hymns; the new openness of my surroundings was overwhelming, the well-ordered atmosphere distracting. Somewhere the lyrics of *take time to be holy* began to dominate my thinking as I tried to gather my composure. This is not the time to lose focus, I recalled.

Suddenly I got a lot of help in the form of one of the nastiest of the paramilitary guards from the previous prison. Without warning, he was standing at my door, nightstick and all, saying, "Sit down!" God, I had thought we had gotten away from this guy and the other one I called the maestro. I wanted to ask, "Hey, where's Abas?" Obviously there would be no toilet trips or water today.

Later in the afternoon I heard some commotion in the courtyard. The all too familiar screams told me it was the madman. Fearfully, I watched through a small crack as they dragged his half-naked body across the concrete and then tied him to the tree. Four paramilitary guards were taunting him with their truncheons and screaming at him. A hush of silence seemed to engulf the opposing cellblocks as the guards alternately sprayed him with cold water and beat him on the bare skin. God, let him die, I callously prayed. But the sport torture continued unmercifully until one of the guys pulled his gun. Delirious, the man screamed for mercy. Finally the guard relented. Then the four guys carried him across the courtyard and out the door. Unfortunately, they brought him into our cellblock and dumped him into a cell across and below from me. For now at least he was quiet.

By dark, it was apparent that our presence was stressing the system. A monk did bring us a small portion of tomato-based vegetable soup and bread, but otherwise there wasn't much activity. On the first level, down to my right, the guards were more attentive to one cell and even gave the occupant a lantern. From the sounds inside there seemed to be a family with a baby. How could this be? I wondered. What barbarians.

As I lay down I tried to recall my entire hymn sequence and was anxious to make up for lost time in prayer. It began to rain. The wind whistled through the open chambers and drove the dampness straight to my soul. At least in the maximum security prison there was no draft. Plus, there was the ensuite, broken or not. I was lucky to have my plastic bag. For now my port-o-bag system was holding. Tonight I was glad it was raining because I could dump it out the window and the rain would camouflage the splashing.

Tuesday, the 26ᵗʰ

It was such a blessing to wake and be able to see the sky. Through the bars in the cell door, through the open skylight, my spirit was free to soar far above. The clouds had cleared and the sun brought the promise of a not-so-cold day. Better yet, I hadn't heard any bombing or sirens the last two nights, but then maybe it was because we were so far out of town.

A tall, kind-faced monk provided the room service that morning: bean breakfast soup, tea, and the special treat of a large piece of bread that looked like a pizza crust. Amid my gracious "SHOOK-ran" (thank you), I commented on the bread. "Like a pizza." I said lightly. "Tell the chef, next time I'll have a little more tomato sauce with cheese and beef." He looked puzzled so I tried to clarify. "You know, pizza and a Pepsi." With that he frowned and said, "Pepsi, Pepsi factory, you bombed—no more." That was the end of our conversation.

By mid morning my stomach was starting to gurgle and I could feel my intestines were percolating. Maybe there was a downside to this more communal living arrangement. For sure, the two buckets of water in the toilet were a poor solution to the lack of water in our building. I couldn't worry about getting further dehydrated—just drink the tea and hope the tannic acid helped.

Around noon my situation became more acute and I felt like I was going to explode with diarrhea. Fortunately a guard sitting at a table on the lower level answered my plea for "WC." After a rush trip to the toilet area, I tried to explain my debilitating problem using animated sign language. I got the same annoyed look and "five minutes" reply as he locked my door. Then surprisingly he returned with two small white pills. Given the immediacy of my condition, I took them both and tried to think about something else.

This more-open cell arrangement and the use of a common toilet area raised the possibility for increased communication. Using my scratching rock and some wet rust I began to mark on a piece of cardboard litter. I thought I'd leave some sort of up-lifting message in the toilet to raise the hopes of the others. Lost in concentration, I didn't hear the guard coming up the steps or around the walkway. Suddenly he surprised me. I don't know what he thought I was doing but he started yelling, opened my door, pushed me against the wall and ripped the place apart looking for contraband. I was just glad he was by himself because the guys seemed to build on each other's wrath.

For several days, I had begun to imagine how we might be released. I still had thoughts that we would eventually go through Wiesbaden like Terry Waite and the other hostages from Lebanon but was unclear as to how we would get out of the country. Finally I settled on a bus. In my mind we would be led out of the prison without blindfolds or chains and board a large commercial bus—something like a Trailways or Greyhound that could make the trip to Ahman or Damascus. Unlike the cattle car that brought us here, this bus would have soft cushioned seats and curtains on the windows. Onboard, we would be handled by cautious third party guards who would take us to the airport to meet a C-141 or, we might even go by highway down to Kuwait. Each time we had moved it was dark. I expected our release to be by mid day to make the journey. It seemed like a simple scenario but it was a lifetime away and thinking about going home was beyond the limits of daydreaming.

Strangely I wished I had a lock on my side of the door. There were even times I yearned for the solitude of the Builtmore. All this openness was imposing outside threats to my quiet and orderly world. The continued animal-like treatment of the madman compounded the already strained situation between the guards and us. As I found my anxiety building, I tried to withdraw to my darkest corner to focus on prayer. My once simple regimen of pacing, time-travel and recollecting of hymns had been overcome by the strenuous activities in the artificial world around me. That night I prayed in earnest that God would put his arms around me just as I tried to imagine he would with Barbara and Timm and help me keep it together.

The 27th

My top priority this morning was to get more of those little white pills. It had been an unpleasant night; I had come close to fouling my plastic bag. I knew I had to keep eating but I needed some intestinal cement. If we could have ordered off the menu, I'd have ordered a double cheese omelet and a pitcher of tea. Fortunately, the morning-feeding monk allowed me a toilet trip and then followed up with two more pills.

I was spellbound by all the activity now clamoring for my senses and violating my emotional space. Out the back window crack there was constant action in the courtyard. The whole relationship between the monks and the paramilitary guards was confusing, and the silent-drill work regimen of the civilian prisoners captured my imagination. If we were to work on a escape plan we'd have to get at least one guy involved in some activity that allowed a better perspective of the buildings and the grounds.

Out front, my bird friends were persistent in endless conversation while they finished all the crumbs at my door. From my own perch, I tried to keep a withdrawn watch on the guards and any activity related to the imprisoned family or the madman. Amidst all, I fought to maintain my spiritual focus. Around mid day there was a flurry of activity down at the guards' table. Doors were opened on the first floor and the guys under us were being marched toward the door and then up the stairs. Quickly, I withdrew to the back wall and sat down as I heard Grif's door open and close. Then a guard unlocked my door and pushed an awful looking guy in with me; it was a crushing feeling. Downstairs, we could see them bring in several new prisoners dressed in what looked like black flight suits and then parcel them into the vacant cells.

The guy now standing in my space was a Brit, Flight Lieutenant David Waddington. He was in bad shape. To begin with, he was starving, had a busted shoulder, and he was barefoot except for some rags wrapped around his feet. Fortunately, he had held on to his blanket. I offered him some bread pieces I'd been rat-holing and we sat down as best we could in the small cell to quietly exchange stories.

David was a Tornado backseater who had been hit nose-on by a Roland missile during a low altitude attack on Talil Air Base during the first few days. He didn't remember much other than they were around 200 feet and going 600 knots on their way in when the missile smacked them. The bad guys on the air field parameter got them shortly after they hit the ground.

He too had been at the last prison in a cell somewhere down to my right beyond the madman. His cell had no window. The only way he knew it was daytime was by looking through a small crack in the wall near the corner. To make circumstances even worse, he was apparently on the end of the feeding line and would usually only get a half a cup of broth and very infrequently got bread. He had been in the habit of taking off his shoes at night and either lost them the night we were bombed or during the bug out from the old jail.

As we talked he noticed my plastic bag standing upright in the window space—seems he'd fashioned a similar port-a-potty. He starting smiling and told me that last night he was sitting by his window when the light rain started splashing loudly on his window ledge. At first he was puzzled and then he smelled the answer—someone above was "dumping his piss bag." We both had a good laugh. It was great to have company, even in such a cramped space. And, he had brought his bowl, which meant we could have one bowl with soup and another with tea. *Wait upon the Lord*, I recalled and thanked God for making things better.

David and I exchanged personal histories and were in agreement about not spending much more time here. He wasn't married but did have a fiancée whom he hoped to marry within the year. Maybe it was wishful thinking but he shared my optimism for release earlier than later.

Around mid-afternoon the guards had begun kicking a soccer ball around in the courtyard. Just as I thought we might someday try to challenge them to a match so as to get a look at the outside, they looked up at our building and started yelling. Then two of the guys ran across the courtyard, out the gate, into our cellblock and bounded up the steps. David and I hit the floor as they ran by our cell. First they stopped next to us and then moved on. We could hear a door open and the unnerving sounds of punching and slapping. Our guys screamed, "No, no sir, no!" but the distinct sound of fists to the body echoed through the chamber. It was the same vehemence I'd heard against the madman. The brutal beatings lasted maybe five minutes but seemed never-ending. David and I just kept our head down and tried to disappear in the wall cracks.

I can't remember what kind of goulash the monks brought us for evening feeding time. I just remember that I was happy to have the broth and David ate the awful looking vegetables. The white pills were working but I wasn't pressing my luck—it would really be poor manners, I thought, to foul the plastic bag now.

The monks did put a bowl in the madman's cell although he evidently had not been eating. From my view down into his cell, I could see he was just lying naked on the cold floor. Earlier one of the monks had opened his door to give him a blanket and found that he had had diarrhea so they just pulled off his bottoms. When I pointed and said, "Help him" to the guard that got me the pills, he just shrugged and touched his head. It was amazing the guy was still alive. I'm sure the others had joined my prayers for him.

That night as we prepared our pallets we felt like we were in the Ritz. Not only did two bodies generate more heat but we also had the benefit of one blanket to fold for the bottom and another to put over us. Immodestly, we pushed our backs together and called it a day.

Thursday, the last day of February
The morning silence was broken by the distinct sound of rifle fire. My first thoughts were that the war was coming to us, that the prison had come under attack by rescuing ground forces. Would the Iraqis kill us before they fled? I stumbled over David to get a quick look down into the courtyard. There was no sign of panic or danger—everything was normal.

The morning feeding was uneventful except that with

two bowls we got bean soup and a bowl of tea. Although energized by the companionship, David was quite weak from being nearly starved to death at the Builtmore; it was going to take more than a couple days of this bland diet to bring him back physically. Yet, how contradictory—the bombing had actually saved his life.

As we passed the time David was content to sit against the wall; out of habit I tried to do some walking but my track for pacing had now been reduced to two steps and a turn around. Most of our conversation that morning centered on the Strike Eagle. He said he wanted to apply for the aviator exchange program and hoped to get a tour on the F-15E.

Sometime around midday, three soldiers walked into the cellblock and exchanged words with the guards. Hurriedly, they came upstairs and opened Grif's cell. Then they came to us. One guy was checking our names against a list on a clipboard. "Come, quickly," he said as he pulled my blanket off my shoulders. Without blindfolds or handcuffs we were hustled down the steps, across the courtyard, and then out the entry door. Oh, God. It's the bus, the freedom bus of my dreams!

My heart started to pound; I can't believe it. It's too early, I said to myself. Instead of being whipped up the steps we were moving on our own. On board there was one military and one civilian guard who directed us one to a seat and, in a normal tone of voice said, "Keep your heads down and no talking." I slid in a seat three from the back on the right and waited. No one was talking for fear of jinxing the moment. Inside, my heart was pounding as though it would break out of my body. It's too early, it's too early—I can't get my hopes up."

The bus backed out the narrow lane, through the gate,

and onto the highway. We couldn't see because the window curtains were drawn but from the early turns it seemed we were headed back to the city. The bus picked up speed and then seemed to go up a ramp like onto an interstate highway—now we were really cruising. Initially I tried counting, thinking I could tell how far we had gone by the time. For sure, I kept thinking, the longer we go fast the more likely we are actually headed West for Ahman or Damascus.

As I continued to pray for God's will to be done, I noticed a used Pizza Hut napkin stuffed to the left side of my seat—this was a real treasure find for someone who has been without tissues or toilet paper. I tore off one panel and blew my nose. This aroused the attention of one of our guards who came back and patted my head.

After an estimated thirty to forty-five minutes the bus slowed and then made a series of stops before pulling over. If the Red Cross is going to get on, now is the time, I thought.

Someone did get on, a paramilitary-dressed man who spoke Arabic with the driver. Then the bus moved forward only a short distance. "Come," he directed. We got off and filed into a one-story brick building. There was one armed soldier inside but the building initially gave me the impression of being an old elementary school. Then, as we proceeded down a hallway to the right it was painfully clear this was another old jail. One by one we were put in cells along the right and the solid metal doors were soundly locked. My stomach turned; my heart seemed to stop as I put my face against the wall in agony. *This can't be it dear God, we've come so far.*

CHAPTER 15

Al Rasid

The cold damp concrete cell was more dismal than any before. I lingered by the barred window space in the door only to be accosted with commands to "Sit down, sit down!" by passing guards. I realized we were starting over again—no blanket, no bowls, new sounds for danger, new steps for water. Even as I paced back and forth, another stopped, looked in and yelled, "Sit down!" My sudden fear was that I would be shackled and lose my only emotional escape—to walk.

God help us, I prayed. Give us the strength and courage to survive. Bless these men so that they may see us as humans too. For thine is the kingdom, the power, and the glory forever.

As it was getting dark someone opened my door and threw in two blankets. "SHOOK-ran," I said. "WC?"

"No, WC!" he bluntly replied and slammed the door.

The good news was that I now had two heavy wool blankets. The bad news was that I foolishly left my plastic bag in the old cell. I had no choice. The right side of the cell floor appeared to be dry so I piled up my blankets and then surveyed the drainage. It was damp toward the front and there was a little standing water under the door. The bottom edge was even rusty. I didn't know if they had hosed these places out before we came or if they were just damp. Anyway, enough research. This would have to do. The door bottom became the emergency urinal.

In the dark the whole place seemed deserted. The only glint of light came from the soft glow of a lantern winding its way through the corridor from the right. Wherever we were, our desperate existence now seemed interminable. I tried to relieve some of my anxiety by pacing but I was soon exhausted and collapsed on the blankets.

I must have easily fallen asleep because the bright light of a lantern in my cell startled me. All I remember was one man standing in my doorway holding the light and the other handing me a metal bowl before he turned and closed the door leaving me sitting in the dark.

The bowl was warm and the contents smelled like greasy, boiled chicken. I tried not to imagine the worse and slurped from the side like a dog. It was food, at least I thought. Then after a few bites I put the bowl in a far corner for the bugs and went back to sleep.

Friday, March 1st, another Islamic holy day

The bowl didn't look any better in the daylight nor did my surroundings. We seemed to be in a portion of the building that had cells around the outside with a corridor and a small open courtyard in the center. There was a one-foot square window hole in the back wall but only iron bars to block the cold wind as it whistled through to the neglected garden area. The wall itself was a good two feet thick at least. Suspended well beyond my reach from the high ceiling was a single light bulb. The scaling concrete walls reflected the same sad tallies—sentences of previous prisoners. Scratched to right of the door, about knee high, were the English letters depicting "Al Rasid AB."

Regardless of the conditions this was it for now and I needed to get organized and create a new calendar. I realized that once again I hadn't packed for the move and had left my marking nail, too. Finally, I broke off a small piece of rusty metal from along the bottom door edge. March had certainly seemed like a long way off when I first marked January 24th back at the old jail and the mystery of the number "43" still echoed in my mind as I boxed in the first of the new month.

Mid-morning three men came to my door. One was evidently the boss, the other had a list of names on a clipboard—no one was armed. The leader said his "men are going to take care of you" and I should "just let them know" if I "need something." OK, I figured it was time to test. "We need to be able to go to the toilette and we need some food—some bread and water at least. And I know there are guys like Waddington who need to see a doctor." He said, "OK" and then said something in Arabic to the other two before they closed my door.

Soon a paramilitary guy came along the cell line dragging a gunnysack of hard rolls. He gave me one. I said, "Again?" He looked surprised and handed me two more. Then he gave me some water from a bottle. As another soldier walked by I asked for "Toilet?" He unlocked my door and led me down to the right to the end of the corridor. Then he motioned for me to go through a doorway and closed the door behind me. It was a real bathroom. Not like the German-fixtured restroom downtown where we were originally interrogated but a modest dormitory bathroom with a lavatory area, four flat-plate stalls, and a large ceramic trough urinal. And, there was running water with a bar of soap. Most interesting, there were cantilevered windows above the stalls that were open. Shortly, the guard knocked and opened the door. "Finished," he directed. Walking back, he held my upper arm and guided me into the open cell before re-locking my door.

I spent the afternoon pacing and pondering the long-term possibilities of the toilet windows. Through my window space I could see my back wall formed one side of a small parking lot that was surrounded by large trees. Larger wood-sided buildings like houses were behind the wall across the lot. This meant the cars were turning off the street where our bus stopped and that our building was only a block or so from a public street. I was anxious to see what was outside the toilet room windows.

Later as I stared through my portal at the tops of the lush green trees blowing against the blue sky I realized how fortunate I was just to be able to see out. My situation was definitely improving. That month in the maximum-security prison had seemed like a lifetime in a tomb. Light was like an aging friend. As the day passed, it too changed from gold to gray and then eventually black. Still, I realized the promise of tomorrow's light is eternal; we just have to have faith. It was easy to understand the verse: *I am the light of the world and he who believes in me will have eternal life.*

I had lost track of time until it was nearly dark. A guard brought me a bowl of chicken parts over rice and without hesitation refilled my water cup upon request. Adding a hard roll from my blanket, I had a feast. With a last trip later to the WC to check out the lights of any building through the window, I settled in for a more contented night's sleep. This was a better place. The treatment was far more civilized and the attention was making the constraints seem less brutal. Unlike other some of the guards before, these guys didn't have the reticent caveman mentality and were more pliable. *Thank you, God.*

Saturday, the 2nd

It must have been the heavy steel sound of the door slamming on the next cell that woke me—then the key in my door turning the antique tumbler. A fresh guard was making the morning feeding round. He obliged my "WC" request and then waited to hand me a roll and pour some sweet black tea in my cup. My intestinal problem still lingered but the tea and hard rolls had helped. Our diet needed fruit and protein, I lectured myself, but at least here we won't starve. We've got all the bread we want.

Mid-morning another stranger and a clipboard guy came to my cell. He said he was a doctor and said, "I'll be taking care of you until it's time to go." Right! I said to myself and dismissed the comment. Still it was an opportunity that needed to be exploited. I told him I had an awful headache from my injury and asked for some aspirin. I also explained that I nearly died from an allergic reaction with hives and showed him how my skin was very dry and flaking off. He volunteered that I needed some cream. Mainly I tried to explain that Waddington's shoulder was separated and asked if he would try to get him some help. He nodded. Later his assistant returned with two pills and a tube of cream. He wouldn't leave it but squeezed some in my hand.

Sometime after noon two civilians showed up in the corridor stringing some electric wire along the opposite wall.

They secured the lines loosely and then yelled at each other from opposite ends as though they were checking the power. It had never come to my mind that the power was off due to the bombing. How ironic: restoring electricity meant lights and would add danger to a possible escape through the WC window.

The next surprise was a blanket check. Two guys came along dragging a bundle of blankets. "How many?" one asked. "Two," I said. He pulled out three more and pushed them through my door. Oh God, it's better than Christmas. I spent the next hour folding them into a sleeping bag with three blankets folded in thirds to make a super soft mattress. I couldn't wait to try out my new luxury pallet. For the first time I wouldn't have to sleep in a contorted ball.

All these new benefits seemed to restore my thirst for more amenities. As the next guard passed I asked for food. He answered, "Soon" so I asked for a "WC" trip. It worked. That night came the biggest surprise yet. With the mystery meat and rice I got fruit—two tangerines—another answered prayer. I ate one and saved one.

Sunday, March 3rd. Not just another day.

I awoke early to the same cold, dark, damp isolation that made this cell just like the others. Loud crashing and shooting sounds had shattered the refuge of my sleep. All my new-given amenities could not replace my dreams of being home. *Good morning Lord, and Lord it is a good morning,* I repeated just as I had each morning on waking. Today was Sunday. My time in prayer had suffered yesterday with all the overwhelming distractions; the endless agony was gnawing at my psyche. At least in isolation I was able to lose myself in my hymns and prayer. Now I could see the outside and it teased me with the world I'd known in a lifetime before prison. Surely, my faith was being tested.

The gray light slowly brought back the images on my cold concrete walls and signaled the beginning of another day. It must be early, I thought, but unusual sounds of activity in the corridor raised my hopes that someone might answer my faint knock to go to the toilet area. A cell door to my left was slamming closed; I cautiously waited with all senses keen. Then the sound of a key and I watched with half-feared anticipation as my door swung open with the same rusty screeching. It was feeding time already. I looked in amazement—a hard-boiled egg, a stone roll with butter and, beyond all imagination, an orange. Something was up.

I scarfed down the egg and even licked the butter spot on the tin plate. The orange was a special treat. As I peeled it, I thought about my morning routine at Thumrait—eating a couple fresh oranges. This was a great improvement to our diet.

By the time I finished eating an extra roll and everything but the orange peel and seeds, a guard unlocked my door for an unsolicited "WC." There, just inside the door, someone had put a large oil barrel filled with water. I used the urinal trough, washed my hands under the spigot and started out the door as I wiped my hands on my pants when the guard surprisingly uttered, "You wash" and motioned around his chest before he closed the door.

For the first time in seven weeks, I hurriedly, yet suspiciously took off my clothes and climbed in. More shocking than the cold water was the pitiful skeleton frame I saw as I splashed my body. No wonder I was always so cold; I had no idea I'd been wasting away. The guard's yell to "finish" snapped me back to reality however, and I caught myself almost comically wanting to ask for a towel. Instead, I quickly used the outside of my shirt to damp dry and was directed forcefully back to my cell. Maybe, I thought, I'd made a stupid survival mistake by using my shirt; now I was cold and wet.

As I sat huddled in my blanket trying to let my shirt air dry, I could hear the others' doors opening and closing in sequence; at least we were getting a little cleaning.

Again someone unlocked my door. Another guard handed me a clean, folded yellow suit and sternly directed, "Put on."

Then, before noon more commotion and another guard opened my door and motioned me to come out into the hallway. "Sit," was the order. There was a razor, soap and water, and a mirror. The guard began to cautiously cut and shave my beard and seemed almost insulted when I insisted on not keeping a mustache. Inside I smiled. His eyes were stern but strangely were not filled with the hate I had seen in the other guards at the Biltmore.

Too many new unexplainable things were happening in my stagnant world of isolation. My suspicions rose, my heart pounded, yet I tried to restrain my hopes. Each morning, since that first old jail in Baghdad, I had focused on the abbreviated calendar I had etched on the wall. As I marked each new day, my mind's eye saw the number "43." Today was the 43rd day since I had been shot down on the fourth night of the war. My senses now strained for every clue as activity and strange noises continued in the cellblock through the afternoon. With each passing minute I became more impatient. The moments seemed like hours. Come on, let's get on with it! To calm the anxiety of my racing thoughts, I withdrew to prayer. *Thank you for the food, especially the fruit, the chance to wash and all your blessings. Give me the strength to carry on—thy will be done in your time Lord.*

As the dismal shadows moved across my cell, my despair grew more intense. We did get an evening meal with more fruit and bread but as darkness settled in, the promising activity in the corridor subsided and the place seemed deserted again. I remembered the sounds that woke me and recalled the reality of my long-held belief that as long as there was bombing and shooting, we should not even think about freedom. My hopes for this special day now faded with the daylight.

Sitting alone in the dark, my determination and resolve began to falter; my strength had been drained by the emotional ordeal of the day. Now on the brink of doubt, my thoughts were filled with a new calm. Just as the 23rd Psalm had flooded my being the night I was shot down, new words of comfort came to me: Alone, I sit in the dark—The Lord lights my way...I pray for the moment—He knows my journey's end...I sing his hymns—He keeps me sane...I put my hand in His—He answers my prayers...Someday, our Shepherd will lead us home.

These words stayed with me and comforted me as I fell asleep that Sunday night.

The 4th

For the first time since eternity, I didn't wake to cold, stiff, aching muscles and my Good Morning, Lord was an honest greeting rather than a plea. I was still alive and the surprising sight of cheese along with another egg and bread on my feeding plate restored my optimism that our situation was continuing to improve. It hadn't been so cold last night and with the extra blankets I was finally able to lie on my back and still cover my shoes and my head. As I ate I repeated the lines that had so clearly come to me last night. I had never prayed for God to get us out of there; it was always when it's time. Now, the phrase: someday our shepherd will led us home reminded me of His promise.

Around mid-morning while I was trying to do some pacing, a soldier came up to my door window space and stuck a piece of cardboard through the bars to block my view into the hall and courtyard. I thought this was a good deal at first since I had been trying to stop the wind tunnel effect through my cell. Then I began to feel closed in again; I began to walk faster and take shorter steps. My anxiety became disconcerting and I realized the same uneasy emotions that I had felt when they chained the madman to my door. After several attempts to dislodge it from inside, I finally made myself heard to passing guard and asked to go to the toilet. Coming back, instead of stepping into my cell, I reached around the door and pulled out the cardboard. "Please, no," I said to him as I placed it on the floor by the opposite wall. He didn't object.

The two civilians who had strung the electrical cord on Saturday came back. Their somewhat frustrated voices echoed around the corridors with determination.

My next visitors were really strange. Another civilian and a guy in a flight suit. They unlocked my door and just stood there and stared at me. Then the civilian said something that implied his companion was a pilot. So, I cautiously stepped forward and slowly extended my hand. "You are pilot, too," I said in an effort to bolster the human aspect of the guys locked behind these doors. "Yes, I fly MIG 21," he replied. I smiled slightly and nodded. Then he smiled and extended his hand to mine. After a moment they moved on. In other circumstances, I would have asked him in for lemonade and we would have talked about flying fighters. If he were alone, I would have asked him about the war and I'm sure we would have eventually talked politics—but not today.

Suddenly, the light in my cell went on and a cheer echoed from across the courtyard. They'd done it! The two guys had gotten electrical power to our building.

The stark light illuminated the ceiling and made the place seem smaller—like being inside an old dirty milk carton. At first I thought about the advantage of the heat from the bulb and how it would take away the dampness. Then, as the afternoon wore on, the constant light became an annoyance; it was an intrusion in my space. I couldn't get beyond its reach. Moreover, it extinguished the sun's shadows and captured time in its spell.

By the time the guard brought the evening food I was ready to climb the wall to smash the light. I really had no interest in seeing the drowned parts of the gruel and I yearned for the solitude of the dark. The glaring single light brought my focus to the confining four gray walls. Even walking was irritating. I now felt more claustrophobic and I could even sense the crowding of my shadow following me on the floor. I was frustrated and exhausted. I wanted to lie down but the light kept me pacing in a small nervous circle. Finally I asked to go to the toilet. Through the high windows I saw lights and thought we may have missed another chance to escape. Coming back I saw the light button outside my door. I pushed it and my cell went dark. "Sleep," I said to the guard and pulled my own door closed as I went inside.

As I collapsed on my pallet I felt as though my own shade of gray was paling. The fruit, butter and cheese had been wonderful and the sweet black tea was really good but I felt weak and was losing my interest in pacing. It had been several days since I did some push-ups.

Tonight it had seemed unusually quiet. I wasn't aware of the normal opening and closing of cell doors during feeding, nor the sound of anyone else going to the toilet. My greatest fear was growing in my mind: maybe I'd been left. I recounted the days. Nineteen from thirty-one in January makes twelve, plus twenty-eight for February and then three in March totaled forty-three. Yesterday there seemed to be so much preparation. And, we hadn't heard any sirens or explosions for a couple nights.

As I prayed my Lord's Prayer I repeated the phase *thy will be done* several times and thought of the verses of Kum By Ya that say, "Someone's crying Lord…, someone's praying Lord…, and someone's singing Lord." As it started to rain outside, I decided that tomorrow I would sleep in and let them wake me at the morning feeding.

Tuesday, March 5, 1991—Someday.

A loud boom like an explosion startled me and then I heard the action of the heavy bolt on the cell door. The guard had a plate of breakfast but I asked to go to the toilet; he nodded. I splashed some water on my face and then as I walked back up the deserted corridor began thinking about having both the oranges I'd saved. The meal was a feast—an egg, a piece of cheese, and bread with butter and a gob of marmalade. In a few minutes the guy came back and said, "Finish." Hey, what's the hurry? I thought. Except for the view, this was the best breakfast yet.

As I lapped the last tastes of butter and marmalade from the plate my door was opened again. There were four guys including an older guy in a clean and pressed military uniform. Normally if I stood, the guard would say to sit but this morning, with this group, I sensed it was OK. I set down the plate and slowly stood from my blanket-draped crouch. "Are you Colonel David William Eberly?" he asked. Cautiously, I took a step forward and answered. "Yes, but why do you ask?" His response was simple, "I am here to take you home."

I was stunned. I looked at him and then at the others. They were not laughing as though it was another trick; his dark eyes seemed to say he was telling the truth.

"Yes?" I questioned. He nodded.

Boldly I took another step and put my arms around him and patted his back in Arab fashion. My cold, hardened emotions began to crack when I felt his embrace. So many guarded days—a lifetime of deception and torture. As I started to break down he whispered to me, "Remember, you are a man."

"Yes, I know but I can't believe this."

"Yes," he replied, "just a few minutes now."

I asked one of the others if I could go to the toilet. "One moment," he said, as they left. The door swung partially closed; they made no effort to close it. Within a minute another guard opened it wider and said, "WC?"

I walked out into the hallway. There, standing in front of a cell to my right, was Waddington. We exchanged blank stares as I passed and patted his arm.

I didn't take long in the toilet. When I came out and looked up the corridor I was surprised to see so many others in yellow suits. Dear God, this is it! I thought. I walked past my cell but didn't bother to look in. Instead I moved on and joined the line that had formed at the far end. For a moment I thought about the two rolls still wrapped in my blanket. And then, the anxiety passed. I had never seen these people; there were even two females. I strained to see Grif and the civilians (Simon and his crew).

As my turn came a man put a surgical blindfold over my head and then sprayed me with some cologne. I was guided out the door into the bright warm sun. Out the bottom of my mask I could see my shadow but this time I didn't feel claustrophobic and I was glad it was coming along—maybe I wasn't dreaming.

CHAPTER 16

The Road to Freedom

I was still blindfolded but I could sense an air of optimism as I was helped into a seat. This time I was sitting beside someone—someone else dressed in yellow duck.

The bus moved forward and then made a U-turn and pulled out the same gate we must have come in and on to a city street. My thoughts raced back to our last bus trip just five days before and I prayed again, *your time Lord, thy will be done.* Within blocks of our prison, a person came down the isle and lifted our blindfolds. He was a soldier but I can't remember if he or the other guard was armed. All those strangers I had seen in the corridor now filled the bus. Guy Hunter was sitting next to me. I raised myself slightly and scanned the backs of the heads in front of me looking desperately for Grif.

"Guy, where's Grif. Do you see Grif?" I inquired.

"No, he's not here," he said. "He was released with some others yesterday—ten of them." Then he looked directly at me and said, "Who are you?"

"David Eberly, don't you remember?"

"God, you look bad," he said.

I continued trying to identify guys from our night together nearly two weeks ago. Everyone looked the same—except for the two women. There were no apparent civilians.

"How about Simon and the CBS guys?" I asked.

"Don't know," he said.

As the bus wound through the city we pulled back the window curtains. I didn't know what to expect. Except for the dress, it seemed like business as usual in any big international city. After about ten minutes the bus slowed as we approached a large mob of people standing along a brick wall with a large iron gate. Inside was a big brick building with a marquee for the Novotel Hotel. Hanging midway up the front side was a large square white tarpaulin with a huge red cross and the words "International Committee of the Red Cross." This was it!

Armed soldiers along the perimeter parted the crowd and the bus drove through the gate and stopped near a side door to the right. An Englishman came out of the building, stepped on the bus and said, "You may come with me." Without fanfare or hesitation we stood and exited, filing past the soldier standing by the driver. As I stepped off the bus I paused by the second soldier who was standing outside at the bottom of the steps and handed him my last two dates I'd been saving in my sock. "Good luck," I whispered. Walking on, I thought I heard him say "good luck" in return.

As I approached the door I quickly glanced to the left toward the crowd outside the wall. They were chanting, but not applauding. Strangely, the armed soldiers standing just inside the wall appeared more focused on us than holding back the shouting onlookers.

Inside, we crossed through a sitting area in the lobby under the inquisitive stares of two families, walked down a hall to the right, and filed into a conference room on the left. There was restrained jubilation as haggard men and women, linked only by common dress, began to introduce themselves. I was excited but at the same time concerned. Grif and the CBS guys—I wished I could be certain they were safe. I didn't understand where the two females in yellow suits had come from either. I introduced myself to one woman.

"I'm David Eberly."

"Major Cornam, sir," she replied and then briefly went on to say she had been on a rescue mission for Bill Andrews.

Then a woman wearing a Red Cross nametag introduced herself as part of the special International Committee of the Red Cross (ICRC) team and said, "You are under our protection now."

"Excuse me, ma'am," I said. "But who is protecting you? It seems like a lot of soldiers outside."

"Yes," she answered. "They are Republican Guards designated to protect us."

Then she went through a sort of roll call. Seemed that just as the Iraqis had ignored the accords of the Geneva Convention as they had done with us, they had also never provided the ICRC with any POW information such as where we were being held or even who was alive. I was sorry that I had never found Doc Koritz or Donnie Holland in some prison along the way or that they weren't here now. For the families of Bob Wetzel and Dale Storr, it would be different. They had been previously reported by wingman as "no chute" and listed as killed-in-action. They were here, alive.

Next, Max-Joseph Meyer, the head of the team from Geneva introduced himself and told us they had secured the entire fourth floor for our use. As we headed for the elevator I introduced myself as the apparent senior returnee and we began a dialogue on the plan for our trip out of Baghdad. Max told me they had chartered two C-9 aircraft and that the planes were to come from Kuwait City bringing the first 300 Iraqi prisoners. They were to land around two o'clock and then we were to load and fly out of the Baghdad airport to Riyadh. Two problems were complicating the certainty of this scheme. First, the weather. Even looking out the window we could see the visibility was marginal. Second, communications. Our release had come so quickly that the Red Cross was scrambling to establish a line of communication with the outside world to verify we had been repatriated. This would key the release of the first 300 Iraqi POWs in Kuwait and begin the repatriation process. Without phones, Max told me they were operating on an old short-wave radio that had been left in the Baghdad office.

Upstairs, most of us crowded into one room just around the corner to the right from the two elevators. The conversations generally centered on comparing individual experiences as we tried to sort out who was being held where and trying to piece together hand drawn sketches of the different prisons. One of the Red Cross ladies circulated a formal list of all the missing-in-action in hopes we might have heard their name or maybe we had seen them along the way. Fortunately, we were now all accounted for.

The team brought some Arabic newspapers and Swiss chocolate and had ordered some bottles of Pepsi. Most of the longer held returnees found the sodas too strong and asked for hard-boiled eggs, bread and bottled water. Later, the hotel chef fixed some mystery-meat kabobs and salad. Soon the most popular and the most valuable member of the Red Cross team was the doctor who had brought plenty of Imodium.

By mid-afternoon it was apparent that the weather would not improve. This meant the chartered C-9s could not get into Baghdad. Max was ready to have us go by chartered bus to Amman like the first ten returnees had done the day before, but I felt it was too dangerous. I was overly concerned for our safety. Being guarded by the Republican Guards was not my choice of protection but at least we were somewhat secure in the hotel with the eyes of the televised world upon us. And, we had taken too many bus trips to other prisons. We would stay.

Max mentioned that the hotel was going to provide two additional guards. Suspiciously, I queried two armed goons who had showed up near the elevators; they acted surprised and asked "How many you are" and about the hotel. I told Max about my conversation and we agreed to get rid of them. When Max called downstairs the hotel manager told him these were not his guys. When he returned to the elevators, they had gone.

We decided to work the security problem ourselves. First, we posted a Red Cross person at the elevators and then unscrewed the lights in the stairwell and positioned a food cart to block the door. I was surprised at first to learn Max was unarmed, but then they were from Switzerland and they were Red Cross personnel.

By early evening I was emotionally beat. All the talking, even being with other people, was overwhelming. I needed to be alone. Max had randomly assigned rooms; I was in 426. When in I entered the room I instinctively flicked on the light then paused—it was too bright. A small lamp would be fine. Still, I was aware of the spaciousness. At first I closed the door, then opened it. Grasping the knob on my side of the door, I decided to leave it partially open on principle. I could have the door open, it was my choice. Bypassing the closet I realized my baggage was limited to my wardrobe. I had nothing more than an ill-fitting duck suit, floppy Converse tennis shoes, and 47-day old underwear. I took my top off and then sat on the edge of the bed to untie my shoes. My feet were still wrapped in the green silk edging from that first blanket. As I piled my clothes on the floor I realized I'd just be putting them back on after I cleaned up.

Standing in front of the bathroom mirror I could see my pelvis area was sunken as though a soccer ball had displaced a mud hole. Someplace I had seen that skeleton before—maybe in an old WWII movie. The skin on my chest hung in folds on my ribs and, on my legs over my knees. Most was still sloughing off the scales from my hives.

There were a few hotel guest toiletries in the corner near the lavatory—a razor and maybe some shampoo and cream. One of the Red Cross ladies had volunteered her travel manicure set; I was eager to cut the two-month growth of my fingernails and toenails.

The hot shower felt great. For a while I just stood in the stream letting water dissolve the big scab that had grown out in my hair in the back. I can't remember how many times I washed my hair and body but when I finally got out my skin was red splotched and tingled from the beating water. Now I felt physically drained. Bedtime.

With my dirty clothes laid out on a chair I pulled back the bedspread and covers before turning off the light. After nearly two months on concrete and wrapped up in a wool blanket, the bed was uncomfortably soft and the sheets cold to my skin. I tried pulling the covers up around me like a sleeping bag but still it was odd to be stretched out. As I lay there I remembered the words that had come into my mind Sunday night. I had to write them down. Quickly I turned the light on and began to scribble. Today was the *someday* I had prayed about.

Someday

Alone, I sit in the dark
The Lord lights my way.
I pray for the moment
He knows my journey's end.
I sing His hymns
He keeps me sane.
I put my hand in His
He answers my prayer
Someday,
Our Shepherd will led us home.

As I thought about how all the activity had prompted my expectations that day, I reflected on the mystery of the meaning of the almost daily reminder of "43" days. Then it came to me. I had been counting the days since I was shot down—including our two days of evading the Iraqis. Today was actually the 43rd day! Listen and believe. I thanked God for all that was happening and prayed that Barbara would know we were on our way out.

Then my thoughts turned to the noises down the hall. We aren't out of here yet, I told myself. The two men at the elevator could have been waiting to take one of us out and the soldiers outside around the wall could quickly storm the hotel. We really had no protection. I got up and locked the door.

Back in bed I was still cold and uncomfortable and hauntingly concerned about someone bashing in the door and spraying the bed with automatic weapons fire. I got up again, stuffed a couple of pillows under the bedspread to look like a body, put on my dirty clothes and rolled up in the blankets and curled up out of view between the bed and the wall. Then I felt secure.

Wednesday, March 6

I slept hard and awoke startled to realize where I was and what was happening. In prison I didn't dream I was home or even going home but simply knew that when I was asleep I wasn't cold. Waking, nestled between the bed and the wall, I do remember feeling like my bowels were going to explode. It must have been the rich food we had eaten or the sugar in the sodas. Anyway, I went out in the hallway looking for the doc. Down in the first bedroom where we had gathered, several guys were still talking, others had just fallen asleep on the floor or in chairs rather than be alone in their rooms. The Brits did cluster across the hall and Dunlop was trying to care for Rhonda who was rather limited by two broken arms. Max had arranged for hard-boiled eggs, bread and jam, and coffee. Before I tried to eat anything, I desperately needed some of the Doc's little white pills.

The weather hadn't improved much nor had the apparent disposition of the crowd outside the wall. Max had finally gotten some communications established with his people in Kuwait City, but at mid-morning we were still on weather hold. In the meantime one of the ladies left the hotel to buy some sweaters and toothbrushes.

Mo was translating the day's papers; I don't recall whether the television was working or not. I was more engaged with Max and talking about our evacuation plan to the airport. Once again I discounted taking the bus to Amman. We would still have to go by bus to the International Airport some forty-five minutes away. Going cross-country was just too risky without coalition escort; I wasn't sure if we could even get safely through the chanting throngs and overwhelming media setup outside the hotel.

Around noon Max got word that the two planes were airborne. After discussing the hotel exit options, I insisted our bus move around to the back, where our stairwell opened through a fire exit, and that the driver park the bus as close as possible to the door to minimize our exposure. With the bus in position, we left the fourth floor by the back stairs and paused momentarily by the lower door before filing quickly on to the waiting bus with window curtains drawn. As we approached the gate the media stormed the bus trying to capture blind shots through the front window glass. Expecting the worst, I was afraid someone might open fire or trigger a rock throwing demonstration. Surprisingly, the soldiers pushed back the crowd and facilitated our move out on the main street.

Away from the hotel the downtown area seemed to be business as usual. The streets were clear of damage and shoppers moved purposefully along the sidewalks. As we approached one corner the driver pointed to a partially demolished building where only twisted steel girders remained among exposed walls and piles of brick rubble. "That," Max said, "was the communications building. . . ."(the first Stealth strike target). As we passed, I noticed it shared a common wall with a small market where fruits and vegetables were piled high, pyramid-style on tables. And, contrary to what one interrogator had said when I told him we needed more food, there were no apparent shortages due to the bombings nor were the patrons fighting over the foodstuffs in the stores.

Farther down the street, the driver pointed out a monument to the military aviators in the Iran-Iraq War. It was a statue of a fighter pilot in front of a replica MIG fighter. I thought of my visitor at Al Rasid just days before and the irony of their apparent role at the start of this war.

We saw other targets as well. Each time, I was amazed at the precision of the strikes. Before the war I had imagined that the extensive strikes we had planned would nearly level Baghdad. Old video footage of the B-24 and B-17 strategic bombing attacks on the German war industry in WWII had no place of reference in this age of precision bombing.

As we approached the airport the destruction became more evident. There was not an unbroken window in any of the hangars or industrial buildings. Limited blast damage could be seen to a few roofs. The complex had an eerie deserted look, yet there was some uniformed activity visible near the circular drive by the terminal.

Our bus stopped along the street curb short of the main circle entrance. Several other buses stood in another parking area in front of us. Max got out to check on the planes. When he returned he said they had landed but we must wait here until the Iraqis deplaned. We were used to waiting but now several seemed anxious—just holding on to get to a bathroom before the Doc ran out of pills. Finally, the first of the Iraqi POW soldiers emerged from the terminal. Each carried a large paper grocery-type bag. They looked well fed; their clothes and faces looked clean. Some were walking close together and laughing while most seemed robotic as they moved toward the buses. Several looked our way as if to ask if they could go back with us.

I asked Max if we would get our stuff back before leaving. They could keep my flight suit and boots but I would like the Glycine Airman watch I'd worn for nearly twenty years returned. Max's reply was short. "No. Do you want to stay and look for it?"

I smiled. "Let's get out of here."

Max directed the driver to pull around the building. The hangars and ramp area were empty except for the two C-9s and some servicing vehicles. We saw the last of the Iraqi soldiers being herded into the terminal. Eagerly, we were pressing to board when one of the maintenance men informed us they hadn't finished refueling or servicing the airplane. I guess I was still paranoid and asked Max if we could move the bus from the center of the open tarmac. There were just too many guys with rifles on this side of the terminal and they all seemed focused on our bus and the planes. He agreed and directed the driver to move up by a hangar.

Finally it was time. The bus moved back out on the ramp and pulled up approximately fifty feet from the tail stairs of one of the aircraft. We all boarded the same plane. On board, we were met by several male flight attendants offering snacks and drinks—seating was open. I sat near the front on the right by a window.

Taxiing out I thought we would never get to the runway. Throughout the infield there were still manned heavy machine gun and anti-aircraft positions. I prayed God would protect us on this final journey. As we lifted off, a cheer went up from those behind me. I felt their exhilaration but still believed we were not safe. "Hey, knock it off," I said. "This is exactly where we started, in the air over Iraq. Hold off the celebration until we cross the border."

Safely airborne and pointed south, the captain received radio word that we would be intercepted by allied aircraft and escorted to Riyadh. First to come along side were Tornados. What a grand sight. Then, from high above, the contrails of the intercepting F-15s. As the lead closed on the right wing I saw the bold BT for Bitberg on the vertical tail and the US star and bars fin flash; my emotions broke. These guys were part of our composite wing at Al Kharj. I went forward to the cockpit to speak to the F-15 guys on the radio. With broken voice I thanked them for coming to get us. To my surprise I recognized the voice of the lead. It was a guy I had known since my days in the Philippines in 1978—"Jiffy Jeff" Brown. There could be no doubt now. As we crossed the Iraq-Saudi border we began to cheer. We were free and we were going home.

CHAPTER 17

The Journey Home

Operations at the Riyadh airport appeared normal as the captain cleared the runway to the left and began to taxi back on the parallel. Staring blankly out my window I quietly thanked God for bringing us home. It seemed so long ago—like another lifetime—when Grif and I had climbed the ladder that Saturday night and then took off on what was to be an uneventful war sortie shared by old friends. I guess he got more than he expected, I chuckled to myself, and our buds probably already know what happened.

I wasn't paying much attention to the comments over the intercom until I heard something about us being in for "quite a welcome." From my seat on the right side I could see several planes parked together including one C-141 and a British transport.

The plane turned right, then left, and then right again to park. Those on the left began to talk about the large crowd of military that was cheering and about all the camera crews. Someone said they saw Schwarzkopf. I had already put together a list of everyone on board and felt we should deplane by rank by crew. This would have Grif and I go first, followed by Cliff Acree and Guy Hunter.

As soon as the engines stopped the ground crew wasted no time in pushing the stairs up to the door. When the steward opened the door we could almost smell the air of freedom that rushed into the cabin. First aboard was US Air Force Colonel Clark from the CINC's staff. He appreciated my thoughts on the departure order, but said that the Saudis must be the "first down the steps" since the Prince Regent was at the head of the receiving line. In our short conversation on "the plan," he explained that we were not staying in Riyadh but leaving immediately by C-141 for Bahrain and the hospital ship USS *Mercy* (not Wiesbaden, Germany as I expected) and that the Brits were splitting off for the UK.

My next question was, "where's an American flag?"

"To our right," he said, "on the tail of the C-141."

I passed the word back through the cabin so that when we (the Americans) exited the door, we could stop at the top of the stairs, turn, and salute the flag. Now we were ready.

The five Saudis emerged to a grand welcome. I followed them, then Grif, then Cliff, then Guy and the others.

At the bottom of the steps I politely shook hands with the Prince Regent and then eagerly moved to General Schwarzkopf. As he began his greeting I leaned toward his left ear and interrupted him saying: "Sir, you may not know we were in that building that was bombed on the night of the 23rd — it actually saved our lives—we would have had some guys starved to death. Thanks." Then I moved on, shaking hands with another ten guys I didn't know until I saw Pat.* What a

* Colonel Pat Schauffele was the base commander at Seymour Johnson AFB. He had quickly joined us in early August and had been my roommate at Thumrait. We had shared some great times during those months before the war started and I felt closer to home seeing his smiling face.

wonderful sight to be met by such a good friend. I grabbed his hand and then we embraced. He quickly explained that escorts had been sent for all the MIA Americans. Sadly, some could not fulfill their role. Together, we walked to the back ramp of the C-141.

On board it seemed like a cast of thousands. Besides the returnees and their escorts there were other several docs and psychiatrists. Either in their own defense or as part of the welcome kit they had brought each of us clean underwear, flightsuits with our own names, rank and unit patches, and boots. It sure felt great to shed those grungy yellow prison clothes.

I can't remember much about the flight. We sat on web seats along the starboard side and I guess I talked the whole time. They had some snacks and sodas but my stomach was pretty shaky and I was hyped on adrenaline from all the activity.

It was dark by the time we landed in Bahrain and I could tell I was starting to fade. We deplaned to a waiting blue school bus and drove to the docks. There was a small crowd of well wishers, most importantly our US Ambassador to Bahrain and a military photographer from Al Kharj. The sergeant relayed the excitement of those at Al Kharj on our release and said he was to take some photos "just to prove" we'd made it.

I don't know if my body rhythms were just used to shutting down as the sun went down or if the defense mechanism that had keep me going these weeks now realized that help was just a few steps away. As I slowly made my way along the rope handrail and up the ship's ramp, I felt like I was about to collapse. On board, a corpsman took my arm as we entered the trauma area of the immense hospital ship. I pushed myself up on a bed as one of the docs came over to begin the exam. He welcomed me aboard the *Mercy* and made a perfunctory inquiry about how I felt before saying something about taking some blood samples. Seemingly with life leaving my consciousness, I replied, "Doc, I got this body this far, now it's yours." With that he elected to skip the tests and called for an IV. Then he helped me undress and put on some hospital greens. I think he began to understand my weakened condition when he saw my emaciated body. Once they got me plugged in, Pat wheeled me to an adjoining ward area where we finally joined Grif, Zaun, and the others who had been brought in the day before.

The ship was very gracious and had prepared to host us with an elaborate variety of steak and seafood. For some, however, it was more a matter of enjoying the taste as it went down before suffering through the consequences of stomach and bowel rejection. I personally was working my way toward retaining Jell-O while undergoing two separate internal x-ray sessions. It seemed most of us had contracted intestinal parasites among our other individual medical and psychological injuries.

Calling home was pretty high on everyone's priority list. One of the major phone companies had set up some satellite phones. I think it was later the next morning (Thursday, March 7) when Pat wheeled me up to the phone area. It had been a tough couple of months; the John Wayne façade was over now, my emotions so evident as I listened to the ringing phone and waited to hear Barbara's voice. Then an answer: "Hello, you've reached…." Unbelievable—it was my own voice on the answering machine! At the tone and amidst my tears all I could manage was, "I'm free."

Next we tried Brazil. I was able to talk very briefly with my mother. "I'm OK," I said. But again I was unable to control my emotions and after a brief exchange, I just hung up.

A few minutes later I tried Barbara again. This time she answered. "I'm free," I repeated. "I know," she said. I don't think either of us could say much between the tears. She shared my feelings—just to hear each other's voice. It wasn't so much what was said as it was that we were now sharing such a long-awaited moment through time and space. Sitting there in a wheelchair with a blanket over my head my guard was finally broken.

At this point I had no idea of the plan for going home, only that we were to stay aboard the *Mercy* for several days for medical evaluation and recovery. For now, I was just trying to hang on to my emotions and recover some strength. She said the Air Force was actively putting together a plan and that most likely we would meet at Andrews AFB on Sunday. I told her about talking with Alvarez the night we were bombed and asked her to call his family in Miami. I said, "The CBS guys weren't released with us but at least (I knew) he was alive as of the 23rd." Barbara said he had called her on Sunday, the 3rd, from London just after they were released to tell her he had talked with me on the 23rd. Then we agreed to talk again "tomorrow."

Friday the 8th

By now I was able to hold down some Jell-O, although I still relied on Pat for assistance in getting to the bathroom. My call home was much stronger; we both had news of the plan for returning to the US.

Barbara, Timm, Liz Griffith and their girls would be picked up at Seymour Johnson by a special military plane and flown to Andrews on Saturday. The Pentagon was bringing all the families to Washington. From my end I had no idea of any type of formalities but I hoped to be allowed to make some public comments upon arrival to thank the American people for their support. We agreed that whatever the setup, I wouldn't look for her until I finished my remarks. I knew that emotionally, "I won't get through it."

Later that afternoon, the ship's chaplain arranged a special thanksgiving worship service for our group and invited the medical staff and other members of the staff. It was a time to give more formal thanks for our freedom, although clearly most had relied heavily on daily prayer to get through each day in captivity. As part of the program, I shared the ten lines I had now titled "Someday" that had come to me on Sunday night and told them the story of the foretelling of "43 days." Several others witnessed to their faith and the comfort of prayer. Our shepherd had truly been on guard.

Saturday night, the 9th

Early evening we prepared to leave the ship for the airport. The plan was to depart around 10:00 p.m. local time for the flight to Washington. There would be two stops for fuel, Sigonella AB in Greece and the Loges Field on the Azores, before our planned arrival at Andrews on noon Sunday. Joining us on the flight besides the personal escorts were Colonel Tom McNish, himself a prisoner in Viet Nam for seven years, and Colonel Clark from the CINC's staff, who were coordinating the homecoming effort, and several doctors of the medical team.

Many local residents had come to the Bahrain terminal with bouquets of flowers to see us off. Their applause and bon voyage wishes further heightened our anticipation for the flight home.

The flight on the former Air Force One was first class. On board the stewards were prepared for all dietary contingencies from more Jell-O, soup or oatmeal to shrimp and filet. In addition, they had brought a variety of magazines and newspapers for those who wished to start catching up on the news.

Our arrival plan was starting to take shape to include a delivery of personalized leather flying jackets during our stop in the Azores. After a hot bowl of oatmeal, I began to work on my speech. Through the on board communications, Tom McNish had coordinated with the Pentagon my request to speak. Secretary Cheney would welcome us and then I would have the opportunity to respond. With God's help the words came easy.

At approximately 2:00 a.m., we landed at Siganella, a planned refueling stop. By now most of us had drifted off to sleep and the lights in the cabin had been dimmed. When the steward opened the main cabin door after the plane parked in front of base operations, we could hear the crowd noise. He motioned for me to come to the door. There to our great surprise were several hundred cheering and flag-waving people who had come out in the cold of the middle of the night to welcome us back. It was wonderful. To show our appreciation, we all went inside base operations to thank them.

Later, after dawn, I woke again as the gear was being lowered. Looking outside I thought it was strange to see all the trees and heather in the Azores Islands. Pat told me we had been diverted from Loges AB and were on final for Shannon Airport in Ireland. "Ireland, you got'ta be kidding!" But he wasn't. Most everyone got off to walk around the terminal. I think it was the first time we realized we had no type of personal identification.

The last leg to Andrews seemed forever. I think the anticipation of seeing family and actually being back in the United States was beginning to seem more real. Still, as I looked forward to seeing Barbara and Timm, I felt a yearning to be back at Al Kharj. I guess I couldn't connect the fact that our release meant the war was over.

Sunday, March 10, 1991. Andrews AFB

It was a perfect landing—on free land. From the runway we could already see the huge crowd overflowing the area in front of base operations. "Welcome Home" signs and American flags were waving jubilantly. Once on the taxiway, the plane stopped momentarily while someone came on board with leather jackets. The cool air sent a chill of anticipation through my body. Then the plane continued toward the red carpet spot at center stage. The engines stopped and the steward opened the door. The outpouring of love and cheering was far beyond anyone's imagination. *Dear God,* I prayed. *Please give me the strength and composure to get through this.* The stairs were in place; it was time.

I stepped through the door and stopped to salute. The waving flags, the cheering faces, and the Sousa music, was all beyond belief. Holding the salute for just a moment, I thanked God and then cautiously made my way down the stairs to shake hands with Secretary and Mrs. Cheney, General and Mrs. Powell and the service chiefs in the receiving line. In order of rank by crew, each of the returnees stepped out of the plane, saluted, and then was greeted while John Holliman of CNN described the welcome to the world.

Secretary Cheney formally welcomed us home and graciously praised our "behavior under pressure while being held by the Iraqis." Then it was my turn. With my eyes focused on the crowd, I began.

"Secretary Cheney, General Powell, families and friends both here and around the world. Someday, and I say someday not Sunday, finally came and we're glad to be home!

God saved us, our families' love and your prayers sustained us, and for many the camaraderie of our flying squadrons brought us home to fly again.

Sir, I'm proud to report the conduct during captivity of the ladies and gentlemen beside me has been without question. Their sense of honor and duty to country is beyond reproach.

We salute the courageous leadership of President Bush, you, and our theater commanders without which someday would still be a dream in our cells.

To those who served with us in Baghdad, Mohammed, the A-4 pilot from Kuwait, the Tornado pilots from Italy, John Nichols,

David Waddington and the other Brits—
across the seas, we hope your welcome is as
grand as this.

I have a few thank yous. First, the International Committee of the Red Cross, Max
Meyer and his people who met us in
Baghdad. The medical staff of the hospital
ship *USS Mercy* who took us in off the coast
of Bahrain for the last few days, and the crew
of *Freedom 01* who brought us home.

And I saved the best for last. You need to
know that those who waited also served.

And sir, if you'll excuse us now we have some
time to make up with our families.

Thank you all very much, and God Bless."

Now I could look for Barbara. She and Timm flowed
out of the crowd to my right. What a great feeling to finally be
together. For a moment all the hoopla fell silent to quiet re-
uniting of our spirits. Then my mother and stepfather and
Barbara's mother joined us. What a grand reunion.

Front and center in the crowd, I saw our neighbors the
Bickhams and the Tarziers from our days living in Fairfax, and
headed over to greet them. Crossing the ramp, my heart stut-
tered from the overwhelming love of the crowd that surrounded
us; my senses tingled from the spaciousness of being outside.

Next, we were driven to one of the large nearby aircraft

hangars for a reception. All the attention was overwhelming. Following the reception, we were separated by service for medical treatment, psychological evaluation, and intelligence debriefings. Grif, Tice, Sweet, Fox, Andrews, Roberts, and I stayed at Andrews. Cliff, Guy, the other Marines and Navy fliers were taken to Bethesda Naval Hospital, and Rhonda and the other Army returnees went to Walter Reed. We spent the rest of Sunday on "free time" with our families before beginning an extensive regimen of hospital tests early Monday morning. At Andrews we were billeted in DV suites with our families, although after the first night most of us chose to stay over in the VIP ward in the hospital.

Sunday afternoon my family sat together in the small living room of the suite. I sat on the floor—it was more comfortable—and just talked. There was so much I wanted to tell them but then at times I realized it just didn't matter. It was over; I was home.

The outpouring of well wishes extended far beyond the fenceline at base operations. Barbara had brought just a few of the cards and telegrams that had come to the house. From across America forgotten friends joined faceless others in a warm welcome home. Although Roberto Alvarez had already called Barbara, I wanted to call his family. The Miami information operator thought it humorous when I asked for a listing for Alvarez; she had several pages of listings. When I clarified my inquiry for Roberto Alvarez, she chuckled again. Seems there was still a whole page of possibilities.

By early evening I was exhausted. The excitement of *someday* had been far beyond my imagination.

Friday, March 15

After five days of poking and probing it was time to really go home. Our evaluation and treatment at the Malcolm Grow Medical Center was absolutely first class. I was in good spirits, but I hadn't realized the physiological effects of our diet and weight loss. * The exams and discussions provided a foundation for rebuilding our strength and temperament; the broken bones would mend on their own.

Personally, I set Friday as my dismiss day. The 336 Fighter Squadron was to return to Seymour after noon and I intended to be there to welcome them home.

Shortly before noon, Grif and I thanked Dr. Poel and the staff for all the attention and then, with our families, drove to base operations where Senator Jesse Helms joined us for the special plane flight to Seymour Johnson AFB.

The homecoming was tremendous. Colonel "Jumbo" Wray had rolled out the red carpet and the civilian and military communities had come out to welcome their heroes home. I was thrilled to be able to say a few brief words of thanks for all their support before the fighters arrived.

> "Senator Helms, ladies and gentlemen of the Seymour Johnson/Goldsboro community, and fellow airmen. Our journey's over and we're finally home!

The last time I saw General Horner in

---

* On Monday, March 11, less than two months from being shot down, I weighed approximately 100 pounds. I had lost nearly one-third of my body mass. To fly again, I was required to regain my strength and gain at least 25 pounds. On April 2, I flew the F-15E again.

Riyadh, he said: 'The road to Goldsboro leads through Baghdad.' Well, I can tell you Grif and I took that a little too literally.

It's hard, in just a few minutes, to thank people. The warmth of the North Carolina sun is only overcome by the love you have shown to our families and the prayers you have said. Barbara, Timm and I could spend the rest of our lives thanking you for what you have done to bring us home.

The last thing I want to say is there will be those who don't come back. There are heroes beginning with Airman Rocky Nelson who gave his life to build Al Kharj and others who will not return.

While we appreciate your coming out to give us this heroes' welcome, the real heroes of this war are going to come home in the next hour and the next few months whenever the 335th comes home. Those are the guys who went back into the flak, faced the SAMs again, and brought about the decisive victory, the coalition victory of both the active force and the guard and reserve that brought us home so quickly.

Thank you very much, and God Bless you all."

CHAPTER 18

Final Thoughts

For most, the trials of the War with Iraq are long forgotten.

For others, the loss of a spouse, a son or daughter, a mom or dad, a brother or sister, or a close friend serves as a painful reminder of the reality of war.

Yet these trials hold lessons of eternal value.

Our nation is only as great as the character and convictions of her people.

Our freedom is only as certain as our moral and military capacity to preserve it.

And, our faith is only enduring as our trust in God.

Some men still dream of freedom, Others have never forgotten the price of freedom.

The families of those whose names are long forgotten still suffer the frustration of the unknown. Their hearts are imprisoned; an ancient enemy holds their dream captive. They will suffer a lifetime with the torment of not knowing.

The Indianapolis Star newspaper carried reports of my status, captivity and release to family and friends in Indiana. Ironically, the newspaper's banner reads: "Where the Spirit of the Lord is, There is Liberty." II Corinthians 3-17.

FAITH

Faith is knowing you are not alone.
It is believing His promise
And it is living His word.
It is having the courage to stand for Him
And having the will to speak with Him.

Faith is calling His name when we face the unknown

It is knowing His way.
It is comfort, it is peace, and in this trust
He is.